When the Breast Fairy Comes

A Parent's Survival Guide to Raising Girls

Stacey L. Roberts

Positive Image Publishing, LLC
Wauwatosa, Wisconsin

Published by Positive Image Publishing, L.L.C.
6311 W. North Ave.
Wauwatosa, Wisconsin 53213

Publisher's Cataloging-in-Publication Data
Roberts, Stacey, L.
      When the breast fairy comes: a parent's survival guide to raising girls /
      Stacey L. Roberts -- Wauwatosa, WI: Positive Image Publishing, 2000. p. cm.

      ISBN 0-9669970-0-X
      1. Teenage girls—Family relationships. 2. Self-esteem in adolescence.
      3. Parent and teenager. I. Title.
HQ798 .R63   2000   98-83069
649/ .133   dc21   CIP

PROJECT COORDINATION BY JENKINS GROUP, INC.

04 03 02 01 00 u 5 4 3 2 1

Printed in the United States of America

DEDICATION

I would like to dedicate this book to all the teenage girls that I have ever coached, mentored, and counseled. Each of you have taught me many things about myself. You have inspired me to write this book. When someone picks up this book, your voices will be heard.

To my husband: I would like to thank you for your encouragement and understanding. Without this I would have never finished this project.

To my parents: Thank you for teaching me that I could accomplish all I set out to do.

To the parents I have met through coaching: Thank you for your cooperation and support throughout the years and while I was writing. The information you shared was invaluable.

CONTENTS

A Note from the Author

Writing this book has been a lifelong goal of mine. Over the years I have seen countless parents and their daughters suffering unnecessarily during the very difficult teenage years. Moms and dads have been coming to me with the same questions and comments year after year. Time and time again adolescent girls have shared the difficulties of the parent-daughter relationship. Eventually I began to see a pattern forming right before my eyes. After listening to teenagers telling me to write a book so their voice could be heard, I began my mission. My hope is that by writing this book I might be able to open parents' eyes to their daughter's world. I ask parents to be conscious of the time that seems to slip by so quickly and, by doing so, to share in a meaningful relationship with their daughters.

Many will pick up this book and think, "What does she know? How can she call herself an expert on raising girls when she doesn't even have a daughter?" These are valid questions, but they are the wrong questions. I in no way intend to dictate to parents how to raise their girls and I do not claim to be an expert. Instead, I am a messenger. The message I bring to parents comes from other parents, experts in the field, and most importantly, adolescent girls themselves. Though inexperienced, your daughters' words are often very insightful.

While doing research on this topic, I discovered reasons for the frequently tumultuous times spent between me and my parents during my adolescent years. Between these pages you will find explanations and insights into the mind of your adolescent daughter that may save you from experiencing unnecessary pain during a time when your daughter needs you most. She may not admit her need for your relationship so, as her messenger, take it from me and the real experts (parents and clinicians) in the following pages of When the Breast Fairy Comes.

INTRODUCTION

A friend of mine, Jerrold Jenkins, author of *Publish to Win*, was running a familiar route with a neighbor one day and their conversation turned to the topic of their daughters. Jerrold asked how his friend's daughter (who also happens to be his babysitter) was doing. Jerrold's friend replied that she was really being a brat. Somewhat surprised, knowing that his own experience with babysitter was always pleasant and that she appeared polite as well as good-natured, Jerrold asked, "When did this start to happen?" His friend replied, "When the breast fairy came."

I can't tell you how many times I've heard similar stories like this over the last twelve years of training and coaching high school girls. During these years of building relationships with parents and their high school daughters, I have seen a consistent pattern evolve between parents and daughters. The teens struggle for independence and the parents wonder what happened to their sweet, once-delightful daughter. It seems that overnight she acquired the ability to roll her eyes at every comment and expanded her vocabulary to include "Whatever" and "Duh" in each conversation. It seems from mom and dad's point of view, their teenage daughter thinks her parents must have undergone a lobotomy because they no longer know anything.

So I have come up with the idea for this book. A survival guide for dealing with the often frustrating period of raising adolescent and teenage girls. If you don't believe it's going to be a challenge, ask your friends who have, or have had, girls going through this stage and they'll tell you like it is—they *are* a challenge.

My intention for writing this book is to prepare parents with girls of any age for the formidable teenage years and to help shed some light on what girls these days are going through from their point of view. I have separated mother–daughter relationships and father–daughter relationships because they truly are different entities. This book is also relevant for single fathers because, let's face it, the breast fairy never visited them. Hopefully this information will help you weather the inevitable storms and come out with a relationship with your daughter that is healthy and secure.

The "Breast Fairy" is a reference to the period in adolescence when girls experience many emotional as well as physical changes. The only other time we experience the amount of change that adolescents face, is in the first year of our lives.

The 200-plus high school girls, moms, and dads that I have interviewed for this book share their insights into what they are going through in what can be a very difficult time. The moms and dads share great stories and good tips on how to deal with this unique time.

In this book there are some key areas where you will have to critique yourself if you want the situation to improve. It is essential to prepare yourself to handle the confrontations that are secondary to raging hormones, insecurity, developing independence, and self-doubt. If you do not prepare, you as parents can be hurt deeply and unnecessarily.

When the Breast Fairy Comes will not allow you to completely avoid the difficulties of your daughter's journey through adolescence, but it will ease the unnecessary pain and help you salvage a healthy relationship with your daughter.

Whether your daughter is approaching adolescence, right smack-dab in the middle of it, or nearing the end of it, within these pages you will find information to prepare you, motivate you, and get you through what can be a very difficult time.

CHAPTER OVERVIEW

CHAPTER ONE: OVERVIEW OF ADOLESCENCE
This chapter helps you remember what it was like way back when. It gives you a good idea of what your daughter is dealing with as she journeys through these years.

CHAPTER TWO: THE BOND
This chapter allows you to explore the intricacies of the complex mother–daughter relationship and to realize the importance of father–daughter relationships. Both moms and dads talk about their relationships with their daughters. Some are "growing" through this now and others are speaking from the clear vision of hindsight.

CHAPTER THREE: THE ROLE OF SELF-ESTEEM
It is rare that a year goes by that we don't hear about self-esteem and girls in a newspaper, on the television or radio, or in magazine. Less than 30 percent of females in high school feel they have high self-esteem. This chapter explores the role that self-esteem plays in parent–daughter interactions and gives tips on how to improve your daughter's self-esteem as well as your own.

CHAPTER FOUR: SOURCES OF CONFLICT
Have you ever wondered what in the world your daughter was thinking when she did something? This chapter gives you a sneak peek into the mind of your teen or adolescent girl to show you where she is coming from. You can also explore what your role as a parent is and you may be contributing to the problem. Fathers, both married and single, can get a bird's-eye view of the female psyche and reflect on their role in their daughter's problems.

CHAPTER FIVE: COPING WITH THE INEVITABLE
There is nothing parents can do to keep their daughter from going through this Breast Fairy stage. Realizing that it's coming is also not enough. This chapter addresses effective coping strategies for parents to use *before* their daughters get to this stage, as well as strategies to use *while* their daughters are at this stage. In addition, you can find ways to look at your own life, past and present, to see what may be contributing to unnecessary turmoil.

CHAPTER SIX: INFLUENCING YOUR DAUGHTER'S BEHAVIOR
How can you get your daughter to listen to your advice? You have been through adolescence and with your life experience you could keep her from making some of the same mistakes you made. Influencing your daughter may be easier than you think. This chapter discusses different ways to help you get through to your daughter and encourage her to come up with her own solutions to problems.

CHAPTER SEVEN: WHEN IT'S GONE TOO FAR
As parents, it is very difficult to know when your daughter is simply going through a phase and exercising her independence, or if there is something more damaging going on. In this chapter you will find warning signs you can look for to see if your daughter may be suffering in silence. This chapter discusses how to identify the signs indicative of depression, eating disorders, and other common conditions that may affect your daughter and gives guidelines on when to seek help.

CHAPTER EIGHT: KEEPING YOUR DAUGHTER SAFE
This may be one of the most important chapters of all. In this chapter you will learn why it is essential to give young girls and women the tools to protect themselves. Early intervention is imperative considering that one out of four women will be assaulted in her lifetime. Read this chapter and learn how to do all you can to keep your daughter safe.

CHAPTER NINE: LETTERS TO PARENTS FROM THEIR DAUGHTERS
This concluding chapter includes actual letters from daughters to their mothers and fathers. See if you can find yourself in any of these letters. Guaranteed, this chapter will move you to laughter and tears.

Chapter One

OVERVIEW OF ADOLESCENCE

It is important at this point to define the term "adolescence." Webster defines adolescence as "The growth period between childhood and maturity." This definition is vague and too simple. As a matter of fact, some adults I know fall into this category. A more appropriate description of adolescence, in my opinion, is one by psychologist Theodore Lidz who states, "Adolescence is a time of physical and emotional metamorphosis during which the youth feels estranged from the self the child had known." Your daughter no longer feels as though she is a kid, but she also knows that she is not an adult. So what is she? Where does she fit? Where is she on this continuum between childhood and adulthood?

Adolescence is a pathway into adulthood where at times your daughter is part adult and part child. It always amazes me that one minute a sixteen-year-old can say something so profound, so thought provoking, only to be followed two minutes later by giggling with her girlfriends and displaying mannerisms of a child. Adolescence therefore, is the often confusing process of growing into an adult cognitively, emotionally, and physically.

Theodore Lidz continues, "It is a time of seeking: a seeking inward to find whom one is; a searching outward to locate one's place in life." At this stage your daughter is exploring her own intimate thoughts and feelings and sometimes she is ashamed to share these with her parents. She is asking deeper questions of herself. Who is she and where does she fit in? What does she want to be? As adults, we forget that we asked ourselves these very same questions at some point. True, some of these questions seem silly. But to your daughter, these questions are important and of great concern to her. Some adults continue to ask these questions; others have settled into who they have become but have forgotten the process that brought them there.

At times, because of a limited memory, a parent may forget that his daughter has valuable opinions and feelings. A parent continues to see her as a little girl, asking such simple questions and revealing such simple answers. But now your growing young woman is attempting to find her place in society, not just your home. Listen to her answers. Encourage her questions. Don't discourage this development simply because her opinions and answers are not yours. If you do, your daughter will be less apt to come to you later with problems because she feels you think she is just being ridiculous or going through a phase. She may feel that you don't really hear her. And please, whatever you do, do not tease or make fun of her for asking what may seem to you to be the most ridiculous questions. This can shatter her self-esteem and keep her from turning to you in the future.

Adolescence is, "A longing for another with whom to satisfy cravings for intimacy or fulfillment," writes Lidz. Girls in their adolescence and teen years are constantly trying to find their "best friend." "Best friend" is a term I hear often amongst teens. What they are looking for is someone similar to themselves, someone with whom they can share emotional intimacy. They are searching for someone to lean on so they are not alone. As best friends, they share their deepest thoughts and feelings. They also share laughter, the kind you only wish you could experience again as an adult. Your daughter wants to know she is not alone in the world. Since she naturally liberates herself from her parents at this time, relationships with her friends are a number-one priority. This is natural, but it may be difficult when, instead of confiding in you, your daughter closes her door when she gets home from school and confides in her girlfriends. Suddenly, almost overnight, you are on the outside.

Since hormones are raging in both boys and girls in their adolescent and teen years, girls may begin to seek out physical intimacy. Boys become a major focus in girls' lives. They may experience their first kiss in adolescence, and on the other end of the spectrum, they may also experience the first situation where they may be pressured into having sex.

Mr. Lidz continues, "Adolescence is a time of turbulent awakening to love and beauty but also of days darkened by loneliness and despair...The adolescent lives with a vibrant sensitivity that carries to ecstatic heights and lowers to almost untenable depths." This particular part of Lidz's description is what I remember most about going through adolescence. I recall feeling so happy and content while spending time with my friends. I remember laughing uncontrollably at times. Other times, though, I recall sitting in my room and crying, feeling lonely and lost. The adolescent can experience these two extremes quite frequently.

The adolescent girl is emotionally immature. What an adult may perceive as an insignificant situation can hurl a teen into a tailspin. She lives in the moment and experiences highs and lows very quickly. As Mary Pipher, author of *Reviving Ophelia*, puts it, "One day a girl will think of herself as a goddess of her social life and the next she is the ultimate in nerdosity." Pipher explains that a girl's ability to handle an adverse situation is limited because she lacks the experience to rationalize. Many times an adolescent girl will display all-or-nothing thinking. "No one likes me. All my teachers hate me. Everyone else gets to go out on a school night."

Pipher continues that an adolescent girl can be very self-absorbed in her thinking and may come off as selfish or self-centered to her parents. Mom and Dad should remember that this is a stage of development their daughter is going through. Parents should continue to remind their daughter to take others' feelings into consideration. Avoid berating your daughter by calling her a selfish individual.

Interestingly, researchers in the past have stated that adolescence is the period between the ages 10 and 18. Now psychologists are saying adolescence begins at the age of 8 and can last to 24. Today some girls begin menstruating at 8 years old and issues in a woman's life that years ago were resolved in their late teens are now still on the mind of girls in their early 20s.

Perhaps this chapter has triggered memories of your teenage years. This chapter should have, at the very least, opened your eyes to what your daughter is going through. You may be able to recall dealing with all of these different thoughts and feelings. You may even remember how overwhelmed you felt at times. Recalling your own experiences during these tumultuous times will help you relate to your adolescent daughter.

As you read this book, I will remind you to look at your daughter in a different way. If you want to communicate with your daughter effectively, you must remember that your little girl is growing up. She is her own unique person developing thoughts and feelings that you may or may not agree with.

Chapter Two

THE BOND

From interviewing, observing, and surveying over 200 teenage girls over the past twelve years, it has become very clear to me that while these girls were maturing, the relationship with their parents was changing as well. In most cases, their relationship with their dads was either comfortable but superficial, rarely discussing any topics with deep meaning, or nonexistent because he was either working all the time or completely out of the picture. The relationship with their moms, however, was very rocky. Although most teens admitted they did not often discuss deep meaningful subjects with their moms, the mother-daughter relationship still seemed to be one which encountered many trivial as well as serious conflicts. Why is that? What is going on between the mother and the daughter that can create such havoc at times? How can dad help alleviate some of the pain?

Let's explore the mother-daughter bond. If you are the biological mother, it all starts with the physiological bond. The child inside you is literally linked to you and cannot survive without you. Upon arrival, a girl is the closest image to her mother. You have all the same parts. Your "sameness distinguishes what a mother has with her daughter," according to Nancy Friday, author of My Mother, My Self.

I believe this sameness is not only shared between a biological mother and daughter, but between an adoptive mother and daughter as well. Both biological and adoptive mothers go through the same trials and tribulations when their daughters become adolescents and move into the teen years. This young girl is so much like you. She will have to endure all the stresses and dangers that you have endured as a female. She is so vulnerable, just like you. Though your vulnerability may be coated by years of experience, it is still present and, quite possibly, well-hidden.

The strength of the mother-child bond is so strong, according to Nancy Friday, that a physically and emotionally abused child who is placed in a foster home with a loving foster mother more often than not will prefer to return to the abusive mother.

Many psychologists will tell you that the mother-daughter relationship is so intense and significant that conflicts with a mother that are unresolved can result in poor self-esteem in the daughter. This, in turn, may keep the daughter from recognizing her full potential—what she wants and what she truly needs for happiness in her life.

Society adds its own impact. It puts an unattainable image of a mother before us all. Whether or not your mother has said, "No one will ever love you as I do" or "I will always be there for you," society implies this to be true. Think about it, if your mom didn't always live up to those statements, you probably became angry at her while growing up. These statements are impossible for anyone to live up to. Yet, each mother tries to live up to this portrait painted by society. In addition, this fierce bond can represent itself as a safe haven for the lonely mom. The image society has created of a mother's love enables these lonely, unfulfilled women to create an unhealthy bond between mother and daughter forever.

Love between a mother and daughter should be based on mutual respect. Your daughter should be able to stand alone, confident of her abilities because you helped her realize HER potential. And when necessary, your daughter should feel comfortable seeking you out for advice and support when life deals her a poor hand. This results in a healthy relationship between mother and daughter.

The Father-Daughter Bond

The bond between a father and daughter can also be intense. Daddy's little girl will win his affection every time. But as the daughter grows and enters adolescence the father daughter relationship changes. His little girl is becoming a woman and sometimes a dad doesn't know how to handle these physical and emotional changes. As a result the relationship suffers and the chance for a dad to share a very special time in his daughter's life can slip away. As one father put it, "All I did was sit around and watch my daughter and my wife argue. I felt like the odd man out." Unfortunately, this man missed a great opportunity to strengthen his relationship with both his wife and his daughter during a very tumultuous time.

Why do some dads lose this opportunity? "Part of the problem is the immense feeling of helplessness that you get over raising a daughter" states Dave Begel, author of *Bringing Up Emily*. After all, the Breast Fairy never visited Dad. Many men retreat from their daughters emotionally and physically because they don't understand what their daughters are experiencing. The sad part of this is that the disconnection can leave the daughter feeling responsible for her dad's distance.

The father-daughter relationship can effect the daughter's future relationships with men in many ways. According to H. Norman Wright, author of *Always Daddy's Girl*, reports that if the daughter is "daddy's favorite" and Dad never shows any weaknesses, the daughter subconsciously seeks out a man who appears to be perfect. She will have little tolerance for even normal imperfections. Mr. Wright also adds, "Girls who become promiscuous in adolescence may come from a home where the father has not been affectionate." That is, disappearing from your daughter's life as she stumbles through adolescence may cause her to seek out unhealthy physical attention elsewhere. "An adolescent girl has too little experience to differentiate between exploitation and affection," states Dr. Julie White, author of the audiotape, *Building Self Esteem in Our Daughters*. Therefore, you can see the important role of a father in his daughter's life.

During adolescence, when the breast fairy finally visits, the father may become uncomfortable with his daughter's physical development. He may stop his physical affection toward her and withdraw emotionally from her. Again, the daughter may think that she has done something wrong and that is why she has lost the affection of her father. A dad must realize that even in today's society where sexual harassment and sexual abuse is in the paper every day, it is still important for a father to show appropriate physical affection toward his daughter. By showing appropriate physical attention toward his daughter, a dad can have a huge positive impact on his daughter's self-image. There is nothing wrong with giving her a hug or a gentle touch on the shoulder or arm or even a kiss on the cheek. A simple compliment on how she looks is appropriate even when she is not going someplace special.

Sometimes a father, because of his own anxiety, may make fun of or ridicule his daughter's development or her experiments with makeup. This contributes to low self-esteem and low self confidence in a daughter, and also teaches a son a dangerous lesson about female relationships. Essentially, it attacks her developing femininity. It may be the father's way of coping with his uncomfortable feelings, but it can be harmful to his daughter's self-image.

It is important to remember that the father is the daughter's first interaction with males. Dad is the first man she may cuddle with. He is the first man to kiss her. And he is the first man whose attention she tries to gain. As H. Norman Wright puts it, "Do not be threatened by your daughter's sexuality." Instead, help ease her pain during this incredibly difficult time. Stay active in her life by attending her athletic events, plays, recitals, and school conferences.

Occasional compliments on your daughter's appearance and displays of affection are important. If the breast fairy spends ample time with your daughter early and she feels uncomfortable about her development, attempt to compliment her on her other attributes such as her intelligence or specific skills she has demonstrated. In addition to these efforts it is essential for a father to show interest in his daughter's life. It is important to strike a balance. Talk to her about her goals and dreams. Discuss fears and feelings. Men are sometimes uncomfortable doing this but to come on guys—she is your daughter. Isn't she worth it?

Use empathic listening (discussed in chapter 6) as a tool for understanding your daughter. Remember that the *quality* of the time spent with your daughter has the greatest impact on her, not the *quantity*. A dad can have an extremely positive effect on his daughter by doing some seemingly simple things.

Researchers have found that daughters who felt connected to their dads in a positive way turned out to exhibit high self-esteem and were able to govern themselves. Women whose fathers had treated them as though they were deserving of respect and encouragement tended to be self-determining individuals.

Dads as Allies

Many of the girls interviewed stated that their relationship with their father was OK at that point in their lives. Dads don't seem to ask as many "stupid or annoying questions" one girl put it. Most of the direct conflict was with their moms. So, should dad just keep his nose out of it and let the females in the house duke it out? NO WAY! This is the perfect opportunity for a father to develop even stronger bonds with both his daughter and his wife.

There are three common mistakes that a dad can make when dealing with his daughter. The first is that he gets too emotionally caught up in the argument. If he sees that his wife has been hurt or angered by his daughter's actions, Dad will jump right in and ream out the daughter because he is angry that she is upsetting his wife. This will only push the daughter away and make her feel that Dad is taking sides. In the daughters eyes it is two against one and neither parent understands. This reaction will keep her from confiding in her dad about other important issues.

Instead of reacting with anger, stay as neutral as possible until you gather all the facts. As one dad put it, "Don't always assume that your daughter is 100 percent in the wrong." And even after you get all the facts, it is still important to remain neutral. More than likely the "facts" will be very different on each side.

Please don't misunderstand. If you witness your daughter being disrespectful to her mother, you must address that issue. Your wife is still the parent and should not be spoken to disrespectfully. However, you and your wife should not be disrespectful toward your daughter either. As a matter of fact, if either parent is being disrespectful toward her, your daughter may be modeling behavior she has witnessed at home.

If you feel your daughter is modeling the negative actions of her peers, it is essential to address this issue. Avoiding this topic will only reinforce to your daughter that you are willing to tolerate this behavior from her. If not addressed, this behavior will, without a doubt, be repeated. Sitting down calmly with your daughter and utilizing "I" statements such as "When I hear you say _____, I feel _____," may work well in this situation. I have used these "I" statements successfully with older teens to help explain why their behavior was unacceptable or inappropriate.

The second mistake a dad makes is jumping in an argument and taking his daughter's side in front of the mother. This action reinforces to his daughter that her mother's opinions or rules are insignificant. Undermining a mother in front of her daughter can have huge negative consequences in the marriage relationship as well as between mother and daughter.

A better way to handle this situation is for the father to talk to his wife   the altercation and let her know what he thought. Mom is able to rethink her actions and decide whether or not she handled the situation appropriately. Handling the situation this way gives a mom the opportunity to smooth things over with her daughter herself or to decide to stand her ground.

The third, most common, mistake a dad makes is avoidance. Dad just feels so out of it or engrossed in his own life/career, he avoids dealing with the problems his wife and daughter are having. Avoidance only makes matters worse. This technique leaves both his wife and daughter feeling as though they have no one to support them.

Instead of erupting with anger or avoiding, a father should remember that it is normal for a mom and daughter to have some rough spots throughout adolescence. It is very common for an adolescent girl to have severe mood swings. One day she may be depressed or upset about something and the next day—or hour be totally fine.

In the case of a single father who does not live with his daughter, avoidance may seem the easiest and best choice because the daughter is not living with the dad and, therefore, he need not butt in. Dealing with mother-daughter conflict this way is easiest only on the father. A dad should talk to his daughter about what is happening and attempt to stay neutral. Again, undermining the mother, even if a dad may disagree with how the mother handled it, will only hurt the daughter in the long run. Do not take sides. This is a great situation for a dad to spend some quality time with his daughter and help her look at the situation from a different point of view.

In divorces where there is not a good relationship between Mom and Dad (or in marriages, for that mater), it is difficult not to use these situations as a way to get back at your spouse or ex-spouse. This does not benefit the daughter at all. It is important for a single dad to remember that even though his daughter may say she hates her mother, in reality, she will always love her mother whether her father does or not. Dad's response to these situations should be to help a young girl versus hurt her mother.

A dad should not think his daughter will be less apt to take his advice regarding her mom just because he obviously doesn't get along with mom. On the contrary, Dad can tell his daughter what doesn't work when dealing with her mother because he knows first-hand how their conflicts become escalated.

Following an altercation between wife and daughter (or even father and daughter) it is often beneficial to sit down and discuss the situation after everyone has cooled off. Empathic listening (introduced in chapter 6) will be very helpful at this time. Remember that Dad is really not trying to find out what happened because the facts may be distorted from both sides. Instead, Dad can give his daughter some tips on how to approach Mom or how to react if Mom comes down on her for something. This is a perfect time to teach conflict resolution skills, like remaining calm and refraining from raising voices, both behaviors that only serve to escalate the situation. Dad can model ways to control anger by noticing the warning signs leading up to an explosion and mastering diaphragmatic breathing. (These topics are discussed in subsequent chapters.) It is also very important to stress to a daughter that her mother may be wrong in her eyes but Mom is still an adult, not to mention her mother, and should be treated with respect.

It is foolish to expect a teenage girl to take advice from her father the first time she is approached with this idea. It may take a few times before she really trusts her father's advice. And remember, if you are disrespectful to your daughter's mother, she will see this and model that behavior.

A suggestion I received from most of the fathers I spoke with was to talk to the moms. Speaking to Mom, not necessarily to see what happened but to reinforce that this is a stage the daughter is going through, can be beneficial to both you and your wife's relationship and your relationship with your daughter. It is important to reiterate to Mom that she is doing the best she can. You can give some suggestions or advice if she asks for it, but do not force it on her. Again, empathic listening would be a great tool to use when speaking with your wife or ex-wife. Reminding her to try empathic listening with her daughter may be helpful, but for the most part Dad may need to be a sounding board for Mom. Refrain from giving your opinion on who is right or wrong; instead offer your support and assurance that you will speak to your daughter about being more respectful. If it is evident that Mom is not being respectful of her daughter, you must gently find a way to remind her that your daughter may be modeling that behavior. Or better yet, you may suggest that your daughter is modeling the behavior of *both* of you. This way, Mom doesn't feel as though it is all her fault. Indeed, it is imperative to model respectful behavior as a dad.

Don't forget, a dad should encourage his wife to speak to his daughter. Or a wife could write a letter explaining her feelings and give this to her daughter. Again, refer to the chapter 6 for additional techniques.

In a messy divorce where there are hard feelings between parents, it is imperative that the difficult times Mom and daughter are having do not become an opportunity for Dad to bad mouth Mom in front of any of the children (or vice versa). It is so important to put the daughter's feelings ahead of any problems between parents and to offer encouragement instead of jumping on the anger bandwagon. Using the conflict between mother and daughter as an avenue to gang up on Mom is only a lose/lose/lose situation for Mom, Dad, and daughter.

A single father who is the primary care giver of his daughter may find it helpful to know that when the breast fairy does come there is going to be some turmoil. This single dad may end up receiving the brunt of the exercising of independence. It should be helpful to know that this period of liberation is normal. Referring to the chapters discussing source of conflict, coping mechanisms, and overview of adolescence will be extremely helpful to dads who must wear both parenting hats.

Chapter Three

THE ROLE OF SELF-ESTEEM

Rarely a year goes by these days when we don't hear or read something regarding the topic of self-esteem and its importance in children. What exactly is self-esteem and why is it such an important issue for girls? According to Dr. Susan Baile, orator of the audio tape *Building Self-Esteem in Your Child* by Career Track, "Self-esteem is a valuation of oneself." In other words, self-esteem is feeling a basic sense of self-worth and a basic sense of competency. A person with high self-esteem would be able to say "I'm happy with the way I am, I can cope with any problems, and I deserve happiness" in every aspect of my life. An adolescent girl with low self-esteem may be apt to give in to the dangers of promiscuity that could result in teenage pregnancy. Low self-esteem could also cause girls to fall prey to eating disorders, unhealthy relationships, depression, self-destructive behavior, and suicide.

The issue of self-esteem became a hot topic after the 1991 research project "Shortchanging Girls, Shortchanging America" by the American Academy of University Women (AAUW) came out. This research brought to light the significant drop in self-esteem which girls exhibit when they reach adolescence. According to the survey, which consisted of surveying nearly 3,000 elementary-aged children (2374 girls and 600 boys), 60 percent of girls reported they have high self-esteem. In other words they report that they are happy with the way they are. Sixty-seven percent of boys in elementary school reported being happy with the way they are. As the children moved on to middle school, the number of girls reporting high self-esteem dropped to 37 percent. Boys dropped also, but not as dramatically (56 percent). Also noted was an even greater drop upon entering high school. Girls fell to 29 percent and boys to 46 percent. Think about that statistic for a moment. This means 71percent of high school girls have low self-esteem. What a staggering statistic.

It is fair to note that both groups showed decreases in self-esteem; but our daughters seem to suffer the most. Nearly half of the boys surveyed in high school continue to feel good about themselves.

Why is this drop in self-esteem in girls an important issue in America? According to the 1991 survey, by the year 2005, women will make up 48 percent of the nation's work-force. If this trend continues, what effects will this lack of high self-esteem in women have on America's workforce? If a woman does not value herself, wouldn't it be safe to say that she won't put much effort into the job she is performing? Or worse, what kind of effect will a mother with low self-esteem have on her own children, girls or boys? Unfortunately, we see the results of low self-esteem in teens on the news and read about it in the newspapers every day. We have all heard or read about teenage girls throwing their babies in dumpsters, adolescents dying from gun violence, and women as victims of domestic abuse.

Where does this phenomena come from? From my experience of talking with, observing, and, in some cases, acting as a mentor and coach for teenage girls over the last twelve years, I believe low self-esteem has many different causes. In my opinion the family atmosphere, disconnection from parents, the media, the treatment of girls in classrooms around the United States, how we raise our boys, and society's attitude toward women all have an impact on our young girls self-esteem.

Role of the family

We will start with the family's role. There is no doubt in my mind that society, the media, and schools share some responsibility, but I truly believe that the family is most important in creating an atmosphere where a young girl can grow up and develop a strong self-esteem. If the family creates an atmosphere where typical female stereotypes are the norm, the daughter's self-esteem can erode. Sons are also taught some dangerous lessons in this atmosphere. By typical female stereotype I mean undertones like, "Women are valued for their appearance, not their intelligence." "A women's place is in the kitchen." "Mothers should be barefoot and pregnant." " You are only worthwhile if you are beautiful." " Women should be passive and dependent." Or how about, " Honey, you need to find a good man to take care of you."

The media, classrooms in the United States, and society can and undoubtedly will effect your daughter's self-esteem. But if she has a family model that creates opportunities for her to enhance her self-esteem rather than tear it down, a young girl will have something to fall back on when the going gets rough in the real world. It is when there is nothing to fall back on that an adolescent girl's attitudes about herself continue to plummet to horrendous lows.

Interestingly enough, the results of the AAUW survey, contrary to other literature, states, "family and school, not peers, have the greatest impact on adolescents' self-esteem and aspirations." This point was reiterated by one teenage girl surveyed. She stated, "I think a good relationship with your parents is one of the keys to success in life and feeling good about yourself." According to the AAUW survey, "A factor analysis probe of self-esteem shows that a feeling of acceptance by peers ranks second to academic confidence and a feeling of importance within the family."

14

Media's Influence

What about the media? It is plain for anyone to see that the media's image of a woman or adolescent girl is unrealistic. If you think of any popular prime-time television show you will definitely come across the typical female stereotype on every show. Many of these women are passive, dependent, youthful, and valued for their looks. (Incidentally, if you go by the television and movie version of the typical American female, the Breast Fairy must have been working overtime.) Very few of these women are over-weight or valued for their intelligence. If we take a look at how girls are represented on the small or big screen we almost exclusively see slim and sometimes, voluptuous young women. These girls almost undoubtedly have the cutest guy as their boyfriend or are chasing after or are secretly in love with the cutest guy in school. Girls who are smart and average-looking are many times portrayed as the "nerds."

A recent survey states that children today watch an average of twenty hours of television per week. Therefore these images of women and girls have a great impact on viewers, boys and girls. I suggest as parents and guardians that we closely monitor what our children are watching. Every once in awhile sit with your child and watch a show that she enjoys and talk about it after. This would be a great opportunity to point out how females are portrayed in the media versus the real world. Another idea is to pick up one of the magazines your daughter enjoys reading. Try to get an idea of how she feels about her body and if she thinks the teen models have realistic bodies. Does she emulate the thin, emaciated-looking model she sees in magazines or does she have a more realistic body image?

Dr. Julie White, orator of *Building Self Esteem in your Daughter*, discusses the effect the media has on young girls' self-image and their struggle to attain the unattainable figures of girls and young women on television, in the movies, and in magazines. She cites the following statistics: by five or six years of age little girls already think they know what a girl looks like; by eleven or twelve, girls decide what their body should look like. Dr. White cites other eye-opening statistics in her audiotape such as, when surveyed, 500 Bay City girls reported 50 percent of nine-year-olds were dieting. Eighty percent of eleven-year-olds were dieting. A young girls' magazine polled its adolescent readers and found that 30 percent have admitted to vomiting to lose weight.

Girls, from their exposure to the media, have a tendency to have an extremely unrealistic view of their body. As Dr. White put it, "In adolescence girls experience a decrease in confidence, a decrease in expectations, diminished goals, and a scathing criticism of their own body image." We all know that women bring this view of their bodies along with them into adulthood.

Treatment of Girls in the Classroom

Let's talk about the classroom. Peggy Orenstein, author of *School Girls* spent one school year surveying over 150 girls from a suburban middle school and an urban middle school. She witnessed over and over girls being complimented for the neatness of their work versus boys being complimented for the content of the material they created. Loud boys were given most of the attention and rarely reprimanded, whereas girls who attempted to speak up were at times overwhelmed by the boys outbursts or told it was unladylike to be so loud. The teacher may not have condoned the boys' outburst and in fact may have tried to ignore them, but eventually they gave in and gave the boys the attention they were looking for. As one boy put it, "I think my opinions are important, so I yell them out. The teacher will tell you not to do it, but she answers your question before the people who raise their hands. Girls will sit there with their hands up until the bell rings and never get their questions answered." Conversely, here are a few of the eighth grade girls comments from *School Girls* in regards to asking or answering questions in class. "I don't raise my hand in my classes because I'm afraid I have the wrong answer and I'll be embarrassed." "My self-confidence will be taken away, so I don't want to raise my hand even if I really know." "I hate when teachers correct you and it's worse when they say it's okay to do things wrong in that voice like 'its okay, honey.' " "I think girls just worry about what people will say more than boys do..." "Boys never care if they're wrong. They can say totally off-the-wall things..."

Myra and David Sadker, gender equity specialists, reported boys "overwhelmingly dominate" in classrooms. After observing more than 100 classrooms in four states the Sadker's noted boys were asked more complex questions than girls. Boys were commended for their academic insight whereas girls were commended for social skills and docility. They came up with ratio of eight to one in favor of boys for who commanded the most interactions in classrooms. Additional research revealed that teachers were more likely to ask boys more complex, abstract, and open-ended questions that provided better opportunities for active learning. For class projects teachers were more likely to give detailed instructions to boys, and more likely to take over and finish the task for girls.

Interestingly enough, when teachers were asked if they felt they favored boys in their classroom the overwhelming majority believed they did not create a biased atmosphere. These teachers were astonished and/or embarrassed to either watch themselves on video or review certain instances where their actions indeed supported the research findings. It is evident, therefore, that this is mostly an unconscious action on the teachers' part. Many teachers are becoming aware of their actions and the further implications of their actions. Some instructors are working to find ways to support learning for both boys and girls in their classrooms. What is your daughter's school doing about it?

Unfortunately, I believe there continue to be many teachers who actually believe girls have less ability in some subjects, especially math and science. This was evident when one of the teenage girls I had coached reported to me that her male physics teacher (at an all-girls school) stated on the first day of class that he would not be able to teach at his normal fast pace because this was a classroom of girls. This particular teacher did not last very long at this school.

All of this data supports the fact that the classroom is one of the first places that girls have learned to be quiet to avoid criticism and let the boys speak. The way girls are treated in the classroom adds to adolescent girls' low self-esteem, and a feeling that their opinions are not important. As stated by Peggy Ornstein, "By adolescence, girls have learned to get along. Boys have learned how to get ahead."

I encourage you to go to your daughter's school or any school you are considering sending your daughter to, and sit in on a class. It would be a good idea to ask permission from the teacher and principal to see if you can come and view the class as a learning experience. You do not have to worry that the teacher will act differently than he or she normally does. If the teacher is treating girls in the ways which were previously described, more than likely these actions will be unconscious and will not be changed because of your presence.

The things you should look for when viewing a classroom are how girls are treated versus boys. Are girls readily raising their hands to answer questions? If so, are they called on or do boys get the attention because they are shouting the answers out in class? Also, does the teacher tend to "help" the girls along by giving them the answers more easily? And conversely, do they expect the boys to figure answers out on their own without giving much assistance? Does the teacher have any pictures of female role models in the class or are the pictures all male? Is the curriculum geared more to recognizing the male contributors to our society than the females?

Society's Attitude Toward Women

It is evident that today's society has made great strides in its treatment and attitudes toward women. There are more women running companies than ever before. "Working Woman," June 1999 issue, lists the top 500 women-owned and/or women-run companies in the United States. Twenty years ago there were not 500 companies run by women. For the presidential election in the year 2000 we may see women running as both democratic and republican candidates for either Vice-President or President.

Today girls have many more opportunities to participate in sports than ever before. Girls' groups such as Girls, Inc. have sprouted up around the country in support of the development of our young women. More men than ever are taking part in raising the children, cleaning the house, and cooking.

It is important to recognize the strides society has made in developing more opportunities and adjusting its attitudes toward men's and women's roles in the family, but what unhealthy attitudes does society still harbor about women today?

In the workplace women get the message that you must be intelligent, but you've got to look good. Women must be strong and able to handle difficult situations without showing emotion, but they must not be a B_____! Women should be assertive, but not too pushy. Also, women should be proactive, but not too aggressive.
Wow! Where is the middle ground here?

The reason I bring this up is, make no mistake, your daughter is receiving these same messages in her adolescence. This can be very confusing for her. As we discussed in the section on treatment of girls in the classroom, if a girl shouts out an answer in class this action is unladylike. If a boy shouts out an answer it may be inappropriate, but he is rarely reprimanded.

In addition to the double standard which girls begin to face early on and carry into adulthood, women in society tend to judge each other in different ways than men judge other men. Women tend to judge each other on looks. Although it is very taboo to comment directly to the other woman about her dress or looks, but women have little problem commenting about what someone else is wearing to other women. A man, however, may razz his friend about his receding hairline or the Hawaiian shirt he is wearing and this is totally acceptable.

It is not acceptable for women to compliment themselves on what they have accomplished. Whereas, it is appropriate for a man to compliment himself.

According to Dr. White, women have a tendency to internalize and blame themselves when something goes wrong, whereas men tend to blame someone or something else (i.e., something external). For example, if a woman is trying to accomplish a task and fails, she tends to blame herself and says she is stupid or inadequate. If a man fails at a task he will usually blame the equipment he used or something external to justify his failure.

If a woman is successful at something she tends to give credit outside herself. "Well I could not have accomplished this without you." "If I can do it anyone else can." Or, "It must have been an easy task." In our society women rarely take credit and internalize it. It is more acceptable for men to say, "Well, I'm just good at those kinds of things."

Again, the reason I have discussed these general attitudes society has imposed on men and women is that your daughter learns these things very early on by parent modeling of the behavior, and by reprimanding or encouraging certain behaviors in your daughter. She learns this from the media and from the classroom. There must come a time when we teach our girls to internalize their successes and show them that being proud of yourself is acceptable behavior.

Encourage your daughter to be proud of herself when she accomplishes something. As parents, we have a tendency to say, "I am so proud of you." This can set your daughter up for trying to accomplish things to gain approval of others rather than internally approving of herself. In addition, it is important to let your daughter know that if she fails or does poorly at something she should analyze the situation realistically and not automatically say to herself or others that she is stupid. Instead, encourage her to list concrete examples of what happened and what she could do differently next time. Remind her that it was not her lack of intelligence that led her to make an error. Remember, as a parent or guardian, you must model the appropriate behavior yourself. Actions speak much louder than words.

Can I Really Have Any Impact?
Yes, yes, yes, and yes again.

It is unrealistic to think that you are TOTALLY RESPONSIBLE for your daughter developing high self-esteem. Your daughter must take that responsibility on herself with your encouragement. However, you can have a HUGE impact on your daughter if you stay connected and supportive. Conversely, your disconnection or separation from her during adolescence can cause your daughter to develop low self-esteem.

Working with and observing girls has showed me one thing in regard to self-esteem. ALL girls struggle with who they are and where they fit in during their teenage years. They struggle with their body image, their ideas, their boundaries, their relationships, their accomplishments, and their failures. The girls who, in the end, come out all right have a connected family and/or a positive role model in their lives, as well as a positive outlook on their lives. These girls have goals and they go after them. All of this influences their self-esteem. The girls who have the most difficult time usually have little or no boundaries and their families are disconnected from their lives. This does not mean that Mom or Dad does not attend their games, concerts, or conferences. It means that Mom and/or Dad are disconnected emotionally and the child has no emotional safety net to fall back on and there are very few, if any, parameters that are set and consistently enforced.

If you are worried you will not be able to recognize a problem with your daughter's self-esteem, please refer to chapter 7 for some tips.

Additional Ideas

According to Stanley Coopersmith's 1950s study on developing self-esteem in your children, the four antecedents to high self-esteem are:
1) Unconditional Love and Acceptance
2) Respect
3) Clear and Enforced Boundaries
4) Parental High Self-Esteem

Let's discuss each of these one by one.

Unconditional Love and Acceptance

Your daughter must know that no matter what she does, you will love her unconditionally. She must feel that you will accept her no matter what happens. Granted you may not agree with her but it must be evident that you still love her.

If you disapprove of what she has done, it is important to let her know that you disapprove of the action, but you still love her. Therefore, if you are punishing your daughter it is important to tell her that what she did does not affect your love for her. You should tell her you are disappointed and explain to her why you are disappointed. Additionally, a problem in some parenting techniques is not emphasizing that there are consequences to every action. Teach your daughter that when she makes the right choices, good consequences are likely, and when she makes poor choices, she must be willing to face the difficult consequences. It is important to impose both the positive and negative consequences on your child consistently when she makes her decisions so that she believes and understands that she is ultimately in control of the outcome.

If you punish your child by hitting her, I would not tell her you are doing this because you care about her or you love her. I think this sends a very dangerous message. Your child may equate love with physical violence if this is practiced.

Respect

You must respect your daughter. As a parent, you must respect your daughter's privacy and opinions. Snooping around in her room and listening in on her phone conversations will only push her away from you.

Difficulty with respecting your daughter's privacy may arise if you had a great relationship with your daughter before she reached adolescence and now you feel shut out. Your daughter's actions may have you worried about your relationship. One thing to keep in mind is that your daughter is not going to tell you everything anymore. This is a realistic viewpoint. Think about it. You do not tell her everything about you. You do not share your problems with her.* So do not expect this of your daughter anymore. If she wants to talk and discuss situations as she goes through adolescence, that is wonderful, but do not *expect* it.

Respect your daughter's opinions. Listen to what she has to say. Be honest about whether you agree or disagree with her, and let her know each person is entitled to his or her own opinion. If she disagrees with certain rules you have around the house, explain the reasoning behind the rules. It may be as simple as "because we feel this is important." But try not to use "because I said so" or "this is my house and I make the rules." Repeating these phrases only makes you defensive and your daughter frustrated. At least if you explain your reasoning (and you should have a reason) your daughter will not feel that you are enforcing these rules to spite her. She still may not agree with you, but hopefully you have made your point without her feeling that you are against her. She probably will just think you are weird! Incidentally, this is a normal thought for every teenager with regard to his or her parents.

Lastly, as with everything else, model respect. If you are disrespectful to your daughter, your spouse, your friends, or the person calling at dinnertime to see if you would like to change your long distance, do not be surprised if your daughter picks up on this behavior and models it. Chances are if your daughter is not showing you respect, respect has not been shown to her.

Clear and Enforced Boundaries

Clear and enforced boundaries are very important. It is our job as parents to teach our children to establish their own boundaries. We accomplish this by setting up our own boundaries and sticking to them. We must impose certain boundaries on our children so they learn what is acceptable and what is unacceptable behavior. As parents we must make it clear to our children what these boundaries are and be consistent when enforcing these them.

*(In my opinion, I do not think parents should dump their personal problems on their child. Your daughter has a difficult time dealing with her own life much less worrying about her parent's problems, too. If you do have a problem, discuss it with your spouse in private or if you are a single parent, find another adult or seek out a counselor to talk to about your feelings.)

I have seen so many girls confused about what appropriate behavior is. If parents are inconsistent with enforcing boundaries, the children will do the same. If they have no boundaries, they allow others to walk all over them. At the end of the encounter they are literally emotionally and physically crushed. Teaching your daughters clear and enforced boundaries will enable them to make better decisions about physical, as well as emotional, intimacy. They will be better equipped to make more appropriate decisions in difficult situations.

Boundaries should not only include rules of the house like curfews, but also should include how you allow other people to treat you or speak to you. After referring a few girls to counseling and discussing teenagers in general with different therapists, it has become evident to me that girls (and more than likely boys, too) who have the most difficulty with relationships and life in general have no boundaries and have no idea how to set them. Parents must teach their daughters (many times through their own actions) about appropriate boundaries. And incidentally, as your daughter develops high self-esteem she will be more likely to set and enforce her own boundaries because she is confident in herself and values herself.

Parental High Self-Esteem

This topic is discussed in greater detail in chapter 4. But the bottom line is parents who model high self-esteem through actions and words tend to pass this along to their daughters. My surveys of teenage girls showed the girls who rated their parents with high self-esteem also gave themselves a higher rating in this category. The opposite was also true.

The Importance of Involvement in Other Activities

Study after study over the last five years has indicated that girls involved in athletics are less likely to abuse drugs or alcohol, less likely to become pregnant teenagers, and more likely to perform better in school and feel good about themselves.

I believe this fact is due to the girls taking pride in what they do and what they accomplish. Involvement in sports takes their mind off other pressures of life to an extent. It gives them something they are proud to be a part of. Athletics can also enhance the body image of a young girl by showing them they are strong and powerful.

Consistent involvement in other activities besides athletics is also a way for your daughter to develop high self-esteem. Drama and other clubs, inside and outside of school, are excellent opportunities for young girls to build themselves up. Parental involvement through attending sporting events, plays, or recitals your daughter is involved in, shows her you are connected and care.

If your daughter only has one recital per year, it is important to make an effort to find other ways for you to be involved in her life. Attending teacher conferences at school, taking her out for dinner, a movie, or some ice cream can show you are interested in her life.

Ideas for Dads

In chapter 2, the importance of the father-daughter relationship was discussed, as well as how a dad can position himself in his daughter's life to create a positive experience that will last a lifetime.

Many times when young girls start to change both emotionally and physically, fathers begin to draw away from their daughter emotionally and physically. It has been determined in many studies that girls are more apt to have difficulty with relationships later in life when this happens.

Staying in touch emotionally by discussing her goals and dreams in a nonjudgmental way and seeking out her opinion on topics, you, as her father, will have a tremendous influence on your daughter's self-esteem and consequently on her relationships with men later in life. You will help your daughter feel competent and worthwhile.

By staying in touch physically, a dad can give his daughter a safety net to fall back on when she deals with the outside world's unrealistic sense of female beauty. Appropriate touches include a simple hug, a gentle touch on the arm or shoulder, or maybe a gentle kiss on the cheek. All of these examples help your daughter form a healthy image of herself.

I cannot urge you enough to maintain an emotional and appropriate physical relationship with your daughter. This will help her feel confident and competent as she enters adulthood. As Dr. Julie White explains, "If a girl does not feel competent in her own abilities becoming desirable and attractive can take over and become a central component of a girl's self-image."

Dad's emotional and physical involvement during a tumultuous time may aid young women in making the appropriate decisions about sexual intercourse at a young age. Teenage pregnancy is slowly declining, but U.S. teens are far beyond their European counterparts when it comes to teenage pregnancy.

Is Self-Esteem Enough?

As I was writing this book, conversations with friends lead to this next section. It seems some parents are overwhelmed by and tired of the over-emphasis on self-esteem. The women that I spoke to definitely acknowledged the importance of self -esteem, but also felt that for children today there must be a balance between valuing oneself, valuing others, and valuing the world in which we live. Showing appreciation for oneself is an important part of developing high self-esteem, but it is equally important to show appreciation for the people around us and for the world.

The concern is twofold. If all we do is praise our children they may grow up with a *false* sense of esteem. For example, if we tell them they are the best artists we have ever seen and they really aren't, when they get to school and are criticized or corrected, the parents look like the fools. This can result in the child not trusting the parents' opinion in the future. A certain amount of realism must be used. When your child brings you a picture she drew, instead of saying, "This is the best picture I have ever seen," it may be more beneficial to say, "The color you used on these balloons is very pretty." Pick out one aspect of the drawing that appeals to you instead of making a generalization. This way you are still complimenting her work but you are not giving your daughter a false sense of security.

Note: This is just food for thought. In my opinion, it is important to find something positive in anything your child attempts to do. And if you personally cannot see anything positive, at least compliment her for trying. Complimenting her for putting forth effort and explaining to your daughter that it is okay to make mistakes will encourage to attempt new things without fear of criticism. In addition, remember (using the previous example of the drawing done by your daughter), it is only your perception that the artwork she did was not the greatest. Someone else may think it was excellent. This is evident to me when I see people paying the "big bucks" for painting and artwork I would not think of bringing home to my house. Who knows, you may have a little Picasso on your hands!!

A parents we have already determined it is imperative that we teach our daughters to appreciate and value themselves. It is equally important to teach our daughters that this world is an exceptionally beautiful place and her opportunities are endless. In this day where school shootings seem commonplace due to extensive media coverage, your child is forming a very different view of the world than you did at her age. A child approaching the millennium is harboring feelings of fear and uncertainty. It is your job as a parent to emphasize the positive aspects of the world and urge your daughter to have a positive impact on society through community service and developing her own positive attitude. It is essential to show your child the beauty all around. Take the time to share with her acts of appreciation and joy, and the simple beauty of a sunrise or a sunset. Encourage your daughter to reach out and help others in need and give back to her community. The best way to show her these things is by setting the example yourself.

Make no mistake, even if your child seems unaffected, the events of the mid to late-nineties involving school shootings and similar violence are having a lasting effect on your child. Whatever you do, do not be fooled and think your child is exempt from the impact many of these events have had on our country and world. Many times an adolescent carries the weight of the world on her shoulders without verbally expressing the pain and fear she is experiencing.

Helping your daughter develop her self-esteem and giving her reasons to appreciate the people around her and the world she lives in will arm her against society's negative portrayal of people and the world. Then yet, at an appropriate age, it is crucial to discuss the dangers she may face as she gets older. A harsh reality today is that one in four women will be assaulted in their lifetime and one in four teenage girls will become a victim of dating violence before she graduates from high school. Therefore, it is necessary to make your daughters aware of potential problems they may encounter in today's society.

Chapter Four

SOURCES OF CONFLICT

My mother is a psychiatric nurse by training. I usually tell people she went into this field in an attempt to figure out her kids. I distinctly remember her telling me when I was in my adolescence that she and I would start to experience some difficulties when I became a teenager. I recall thinking, "No way, that will never happen." You see, my mom was my coach and my role model. (As a matter of fact, she still is today.) She cared for her bedridden mother since she was in her early teens, stayed at home to raise her kids and then went to school to become a registered nurse. I looked up to her and loved her. How could things change?

Fast-forward a few years, to an evening when I came home from high school. I was sixteen years old. My mom was doing the dishes (probably because one of my brothers or I conveniently forgot to do them after dinner) and we began to argue. About what, I don't remember. The argument escalated and I began to be very defensive and very sharp with my tongue. We were never allowed to swear in our house so I know I did not use profanity, but I wasn't lacking sarcasm. All of a sudden, in the middle of the "discussion," I looked across the kitchen, and saw my mom's shoulders drop. Her back was turned to me so I couldn't see her face, but I could tell by her cracked voice that she was crying. (The only other time I had seen my mom cry was at her own mother's funeral when I was six years old.) I remember feeling a tremendous amount of guilt, but I wasn't able to express it in words. I just walked out of the room without a word and sank into my bed. How could I say those things? I didn't mean to hurt her. But I did, very badly.

While I was researching this book, I sat down with my mom and asked her a few questions. I asked her if she remembered that day and she said she did. I asked her if she remembers what I said and she told me, "Not exactly, but I remember it was something to the effect that you hated me." I was shocked. Never in my life had I ever said that I hated her. But hatred was her perception of what I said and did throughout my teenage years. Yet, even though I acted that way toward her, she still loved me and never stopped showing it.

Why did I act that way toward my mother? Why does your daughter verbally attack you or roll her eyes when you give your opinion? Or why do you not have a relationship with your daughter at all? This chapter discusses the sources of conflict between parents and their daughter. As you will see, even though it seems like it, the conflicts did not just happen one day. There are many situations leading up to the conflicts and many factors that contribute to them. I ask you to open your hearts and your minds and ask yourself some pretty serious self-analytical questions to help you come up with answers for your situation.

The goal of this chapter is not to cast blame on anyone, but instead to allow you to examine yourself and where your daughter is coming from. This chapter will allow you to take yourself back to the time of your adolescent and teenage years. You will be able to recognize feelings that you had and you will be able to leave behind any negative influences from your parents and follow through with any positive experiences. It is your responsibility now to raise your daughter. The past will not define how you will accomplish this feat unless you let it.

See if you can identify the feelings you had way back when. Moms especially may find that some of the feelings of turmoil your daughter is experiencing are the same feelings of turmoil you felt when you were a teenager or adolescent.

You may also notice in this chapter that more often than not I am referring to conflicts that are more likely to occur between the mother and the daughter. This will give Dad a very valuable birds-eye view of the dynamics going on between his wife and his daughter. It will also set him up in a key position that we will discuss in chapter 4.

Conflicts

Separation Versus Liberation
The goal of this book is to aid parents in raising girls. Do I think that by reading this you will totally avoid any problems with your adolescent or teenage daughter? Absolutely not! But you can decrease the unnecessary pain and suffering you go through by understanding a little bit more about yourself and your daughter.

First, we'll start with your daughter. There will be a period of time when your daughter will need to liberate herself from her parents, especially her mother. For boys it appears to be somewhat uneventful apparently because society accepts the fact that the son should separate himself from his parents and learn to be independent. When he is quiet and not expressing his feelings we think everything is okay. But slowly we are finding that our boys are suffering in silence because of the stigma society has placed on them to be strong and independent, unable to express their true feelings. Think about it. If a man is living with his mother or parents after a certain age, in the back of our mind we think, "What's wrong with him? Does he still need to be around his mom because he can't take care of himself?" If a woman is living with her parents, we are not so quick to judge. We might even assume it is completely normal for the daughter to be living in her parents' home. One common assumption we make is that she is staying there to save money before she gets married.

Most of the references I have read have described adolescence and the teenage years as a time when children need to "separate" from the parents. I believe liberation is a more appropriate word. Separation as defined by Webster is "To disconnect, to set or keep apart," whereas liberation is defined as "To set free from bondage or restraint." You may think this is just semantics, but separation implies no further connection with the parent. Psychologists in the past have thought separation will somehow foster independence. I disagree. This, in fact, will make children more dependent upon you in the future. Cutting them off and throwing them to the wolves in the real world to fend for themselves without anyone or anything to fall back on creates many problems for these individuals in the future. Allowing our children to make mistakes, take responsibility for these mistakes, and learn from them is what fosters independence later in life. Liberation, or the ability to "free" someone implies that you are not disconnecting completely, but are giving them the freedom to become who they are with your experience and your support behind them.

The reason I feel so strongly about this is, in surveying teenage girls, over 80 percent felt it is important to have a good relationship with their parents now, and 90 percent reported it was important to have a strong relationship with their parents in the future. These girls don't want to be disconnected from their parents. They want to be given enough freedom to develop who they are, but they need support and someone to fall back on when necessary. Separation implies that there is nothing there to fall back on. They are all alone. In the words of Elizabeth Debold, Marie Wilson, and Idelisse Malave, authors of *Mother Daughter Revolution*, "Connection, not separation, keeps girls strong and whole."

Therefore, as your daughter liberates herself from you, she is establishing her own identity. You may say something is black and she will say it's white. This is your daughter's way of showing you she has her own opinion and it may not be the same as yours. This phase is normal, healthy, and for the most part, unavoidable. Admittedly, it may make you crazy at times but there are ways to minimize the feelings of rejection felt by the parent that oftentimes follows these confrontations. We will discuss many such ways in chapter 5.

The Need for Privacy

Privacy is a huge issue with girls as they wrestle through their teenage years. You want to know what is going on in their lives and they just want to be left alone. As a parent, this can be very frustrating. It seems the more questions you ask, the fewer answers you receive. The parents with whom I spoke felt as if they were being cast aside, as if they were no longer important in their child's eyes. The teens I've interviewed say they just want to figure some things out for themselves. They don't want input from their parents unless they ask their parents for input. Most often though, parents give input without prompting from their daughters. This may be appropriate in situations where there is a safety issue, but when parents try to pry information out of their daughters about what is wrong, this is a big mistake. It will push them further away.

Understandably though, in this day and age it can be very worrisome when your daughter comes home from school day after day and locks herself in her room. She may talk for hours on the phone with her friends, but doesn't give you the time of day. Incidentally, talking on the phone is common for teenage girls. During this time period the phone may become an extension of her ear. According to John Gray, author of *Men Are From Mars, Women Are From Venus*, one explanation for this telephone dependency is that, "it is very common for women to work through their problems by talking about them. Women tend to talk about problems to understand the problem, or quite possibly to forget the problem." For many moms this statement rings true even in adulthood. So, the bottom line is DON'T TAKE IT SO PERSONALLY! If you are extremely hurt by this you may want to investigate why it bothers you so much. More often than not you are afraid your daughter is growing away from you and doesn't need you anymore. This can be devastating for a mother who has nothing else but her children.

How do you tell if your daughter's need for privacy is simply her being a teenager or if something more serious is going on? Chapter 6 will give you some great techniques to get your daughter to confide in you without you having to ask so many questions. We also discuss signs you can look for to see if your child is suffering from more serious conditions such as depression, eating disorders, or drug and alcohol abuse in chapter 7.

My Parents Are Human. Wow, What a Concept!

Every parent remembers her child's first steps and how the toddler would run at them giggling and smiling. You were the center of their world. So, what happens? When and why do they turn on you? A stay-at-home mom or dad is the only source of knowledge and care. A parent who works or a single parent is the primary caregiver outside of working hours. Either way, your child needs you and loves you with every fiber of her being.

The shift comes when she has other influences, such as friends, teachers, and society at large. Your daughter begins to notice your shortcomings and every mistake that you make. You have betrayed her. You are not perfect and she can be very angry with you. During her teenage years, as we have discussed, she is trying to liberate herself from you, and your flaws make it a bit easier to do so. She will challenge anything about you; your clothes, your hair, your ideas, your life, anything to establish that she is not you.

My mother always says, "No matter what I would say, you would say the opposite. But if one of your friends agreed with me, all of a sudden you could see that I was right after all." That may have been true, but I would never have admitted to my mom that she was right when I was a teenager.

A parent's job is tough. Undoubtedly the hardest job in the world. And as I alluded to before, Mom probably gets the brunt of it most of the time. A single parent has no respite; mother or father, they get it all of the time. I really think all parents deserve a medal, but single parents, they deserve a Purple Heart.

**The next sections are devoted to helping you explore yourself and your actions that are creating unnecessary conflict, or what you are doing that may be lessening the conflicts. It is important to look at yourself and see where you stand. If changes need to be made, this is the time to be honest with yourself and make them. This will only help to influence your daughter's behavior in a positive way. As Harriet Lerner, Ph.D., and author of *The Mother Dance* states, "Our kids are the major benefactors of the work we do on ourselves."

Parents' Self-Esteem

Although we have covered the role that your daughter's self-esteem plays during this period in her life in another chapter, I want to point out in this section the importance of the parents' self esteem and how it may influence the child's self-esteem. According to Stanley Coopersmith's 1950s longitudinal study that observed thousands of children over many years, four antecedents of high self-esteem were documented. As discussed in chapter 3, the four antecedents are:
1) Unconditional Love and Acceptance
2) Respect
3) Clear and Enforced Boundaries or Limits
4) Parental High Self-Esteem

What Mr. Coopersmith found was that the parents' feelings and opinions about themselves and how they convey those feelings both verbally and nonverbally are key contributors to their daughters' attainment of high self-esteem.

*NOTE: As you read though these conflicts, see if you can identify with any of them or if you are witnessing them taking place in your own home with your spouse. Once you identify what the problem may be, you are that much closer to dealing with it. The chapter on coping will give you different options in dealing with these conflicts.

As we discussed in the previous chapter, Dr. Susan Baile defines self-esteem in her audio series, *Building Self-Esteem in Your Child,* as "a valuation of oneself." It is a feeling. It is feeling that you are basically okay. That who you are inside is okay."

Ask yourself this question. Do you feel that YOU are okay? If not, I can guarantee that you WILL convey this message to your child. If you walk around every day in front of your daughter and say "I'm fat," "I'm stupid," or "I can't do that," your child will hear these negative comments and, without even realizing it, she will internalize it. For example, I have a friend who makes negative comments about how she looks and remarks frequently that she is incapable. One day she and I were talking about kids and self-esteem and she mentioned to me that she was worried about her daughter. Apparently her daughter, who was seven at the time, was worried that she looked fat. Now why is a seven-year-old worried or even aware of looking fat? Let me point out, this girl had never been in day care and had spent very little time in front of the television. Year after year she had heard her mom make negative comments about her own body. Who does this little girl identify with the most? Who is the center of her world? And how do you think she is going to feel about herself when she gets out in society and is bombarded with all the airbrushed thin supermodels in magazines and on television? As parents we must stop berating ourselves in front of our children. Most of us don't even realize we do this. All I can say is we better start listening to ourselves because our children carry these comments with them into adolescence and in some cases, even adulthood.

Another example is the parent who is constantly saying, "Oh, I could never do that." Or, "I'm just stupid." Again, your young daughter internalizes these comments and starts believing them about herself. She becomes less apt to take a risk for fear she will look stupid, or because she feels incapable.

These are just two examples of how you can effect your daughter's self esteem in a negative way as she is growing closer to adolescence. On the contrary, if you are aware of what you are saying and how you feel about yourself, you can have a huge positive impact on your daughter's self-esteem. Remember, it is never too late to change, whether your daughter is eight or eighteen, eliminating negative self-talk will not only help your daughter, it will help you.

Modeling high self esteem for your daughter, showing her respect (not just expecting it from her), and showing her unconditional love and acceptance while setting and enforcing appropriate limits and boundaries are proven ways to start your daughter on the path to valuing herself.

Preferential Treatment and Double Standards

Do you treat your sons differently than your daughters? Giving preferential treatment to boys in the classroom is very evident according to the AAUW study. This is true with both male and female teachers. In the classroom boys are encouraged more and called on more and are rewarded with attention when rowdy or rambunctious while girls are told it's not ladylike to speak up or be rowdy. Does this happen at home?

It's the old double standard and answering, "that's the way it is" or "boys will be boys" can really add fuel to the already blazing fire. In defense of parents, often the double standard occurs because parents want to keep their daughter safe. In these situations it is important to explain to your daughter why you are treating her differently than her brother. The old "because I said so" doesn't fly anymore because kids need to understand. Undoubtedly, girls will fight against this standard either verbally or by internalizing (girls tend to internalize unexpressed emotions, boys tend to act out externally with violence) because their limited life experience looks at it simply as not being fair. They have very little concept of the dangers of rape, assault, pressured sex, or teenage pregnancy unless it has happened to their friends or to themselves. Therefore, adolescents or teenagers may respond with anger toward these limits placed upon them. This expression of anger does not mean you change your mind on the subject. On the contrary, explaining your position adds credibility to your actions. I believe this technique works especially well with older adolescents. Younger adolescents or preadolescents need to understand that no means no.

Just be aware that by telling your daughter that she can't do something that her brother is able to do, you create a feeling that you are a traitor, especially in the mother daughter relationships. Her perception is that you don't understand, that you are trying to hold her back, and ultimately, that you don't love or support her. This is why it is important to let her know why you are putting limits on her. In some instances you can give your daughter the opportunity to explain to you why a certain situation would not jeopardize her safety. This way she can problem-solve and begin to think of ways to keep herself safe. This is good practice for her as she gets older.

Notably, you can effect your daughter's belief in herself and her abilities when the double standard exists for reasons other than safety concerns. For example, if your daughter approaches you and tells you she wants to be an electrician and your response is "Honey, that's a man's job. Why don't you think about being a schoolteacher," this inadvertently tells her that there are limits. By discouraging her, you are essentially telling her that regardless of her abilities and goals, because she is a woman, her options are limited.

One real-life example of the best way to handle this situation was described to me at a seminar I attended. An African American woman in her late-thirties to mid-forties told the instructor about a time when she was an adolescent. She and her father were riding in the car and she told her father that she wanted to be a high-ranking officer in the Navy when she grew up. At that time women were not allowed in the Navy and very few African Americans were enlisted. Realistically, at that time, if her father had told her that the Navy was just for men and she should think about doing something else, her father would have been telling her the truth. He would have also taught her how to put limits on herself and her dreams. But instead he encouraged her and never once made her feel as if she was not able to achieve it. Today, this woman *is* one of the highest-ranking female officers in the Navy and has several security clearances. Imagine how her life would have been different if she had believed she never had the chance. Your words of encouragement, as well as discouragement, have a great effect on your daughter.

Unconscious Anger

As an adolescent grows older and tries to establish her own identity, she often looks at her mom's life and asks herself the question, "Is that what I want to be doing when I'm a mom, or when I'm old (as they would put it)?" Depending on her answer, this can be a great source of conflict.

The daughters that I interviewed who did not want to be like their mom more frequently than not were not supportive of their mother's situation at home. Seventy percent of these girls said when they get married it's going to more of a 50/50 split when it comes to taking care of the home. Another girl told me she would not let her husband talk to her the way her father talks to her mother, or, in another case, the way her mom's boyfriend talked to her mom. One young girl wrote, "I wish my mom had her own ideas. All of her thoughts are what my dad thinks." They feel that it is unfair that their moms work all day (in or out of the home) and in the evening have to take care of the kids and cook dinner while dads watch television and read the newspaper.

This anger, which you would think would be directed toward their dad is often unconsciously directed toward their mom. As Debold, Wilson, and Malave, authors of *Mother Daughter Revolution*, put it, "A mother's inferiority angers her daughter because it strips her of her power as well." According to Debold, Wilson, and Malave, when the daughter sees the mother "disempowered" in a situation they will continually question her authority.

In one case, when Sandy (name has been changed to protect her identity) was growing up, she remembers feeling very angry with both her mother and her father. Sandy's most vivid memory is her dad telling her when she was a young girl that she should help her mother more around the house. Sandy remembers thinking, "Why are you telling me this? Mom does everything and you do not help her." Her father's inconsistency or "do as I say, not as I do" message, infuriated her. She never expressed this anger toward her father verbally. According to Sandy, there was no way she would confront her father. Instead, she took it out on her mother. Sandy was not happy with the arrange-

34

ment they had made where Mom cooks, cleans, and raises the kids, and dad comes home from work expecting to be waited on. Through her youthful eyes she saw her mother giving everything and not getting much in return. It angered her that her mother would allow this to happen to herself. She remembers that fights broke out between her and her mom for seemingly no reason at all. No matter what her mother said, Sandy recalls disagreeing with her to most likely "prove I was different than her." In her dad's defense though, this situation was very commonplace back then.

Unconscious anger can eat away at the relationship with your daughter. Most likely, your daughter has no idea she harbors these feelings. If your daughter frequently seems very angry with you for no apparent reason, more times than not, there is an underlying reason. In chapter 5 and 6 you will find techniques to help you deal with these situations and uncover what may really be behind the anger. This can be an important learning experience for both you and your daughter. Revealing the problem and working it out will bring you closer than you could ever imagine.

Divorce

Another reason for unconscious anger could be divorce. Everyone has heard in the news that 50 percent or more of marriages end in divorce. Some statistical analysts say it is even greater than 50 percent. Many of these divorced couples have children. These children try to cope with the fact that their parents are not together and on the outside they may or may not seem fine. But on the inside, subconsciously even, these children are angry, fearful, and confused. These children are angry that their parents did this to them. They are fearful that the divorce was somehow their fault. And they are confused about what a loving relationship really is. In time, with the support of both parents these children will heal. But for the daughters, who are already going through the inevitable liberation period, a divorce situation may escalate the feelings of anger toward their parents.

Most of the girls who I spoke with whose parents are divorced say they tend to take this anger out on the parent with whom they spend most of their time. And in two particular cases where custody was pretty close to an even split, the girls both reported they definitely take their anger out more often on their mom. These girls admit picking fights for no reason. "I become very defensive after anything that Mom says," was one response.

Do these two girls blame their moms for the divorce? That question was very difficult for the girls to answer. At this point in their teenage lives, both girls were unsure if they blamed their moms or if their moms were simply the easiest target for their hurt and anger. They seemed to know their moms would always love them even if they were rebellious. When I asked them if they felt guilty about treating their parents this way, the girls both responded, "yes, sometimes." One young lady described it like this, "Well, you know it's like, at the time, I'm so mad that I forget how mean I am acting. Sometimes I'll blow up at her for asking how my day is and I don't know why I do that." Again, this may be common for any teenage girl to act this way occasionally, but if a pattern is beginning and this anger is frequent, it is definitely time to get to the bottom of it.

Younger girls may deal with the anger from the divorce in a similar fashion but are not yet quite sure of what is happening. As a matter of fact, in one particular case the ten-year-old girl I spoke to really did not think there was any problem between her and her mom. When I spoke to her mother, I heard a very different story. Frequent disagreements, shouting matches, and very hurt feelings seemed to be what the mother was experiencing. I am not quite sure if her daughter was too embarrassed or ashamed to admit she was having these angry feelings toward her mother, or if at this point in a girl's development she is not able to process the reasons behind these angry outbursts.

Nevertheless, it is imperative to look deeper for the reasons which may explain the consistent outbursts of anger. Yes, it may be due to her exercising her liberation muscle or there may be something deeper troubling your daughter. It is also very important to remember that your daughter does not feel good about how she treats you when she is angry. Remember she does not hate you. She needs your help, probably more now than ever.

Feeling guilty about your divorce may keep you from facing the truth that your daughter is angry with you. Just remember, avoiding the truth will not make it go away. The decision you made with your spouse has consequences, both good and bad. If you let this go and do not deal with your daughter's anger now, it will escalate and feelings may be hurt more deeply. You will hurt your daughter far more if you avoid getting to the bottom of her anger because you are afraid to face it yourself. Most times asking your child if she is okay will result in the answer, "Yeah, I'm fine." As a parent you must go deeper and be more creative by playing games and having them draw their feelings. This works well with younger adolescents. Teenagers would be more apt to open up during one-on-one time or in a letter.

By helping your daughter understand why she has these feelings of anger and letting her know that anger is a normal emotion but there are much healthier and less hurtful ways of expressing it, you will become closer and form a more solid relationship. As I stated earlier, chapters 5 and 6 are good resources, but if you think that you need additional help, seek out a counselor that deals with teenage and adolescent girls. The school guidance counselor may also be a good place to start.

Trouble with Friends at School

A possible source of your daughter's mood swings could be related to problems that she is experiencing with friends at school. For girls (and women for that matter), relationships are very important. Our lives revolve around our relationships. If something is going awry at school you may be the target of her displaced anger.

Sometimes when a girl is too afraid to express her true feelings of anger toward her friends or even teachers, she internalizes this anger. That is, until you happen to ask her how her day was and then she lets you have it. Your daughter may feel it is too risky to tell her friend how she really feels, so she takes out her feelings on someone who is safe. Someone she normally doesn't have to worry about not loving or caring for her if she expresses her anger.

If you feel you are getting the brunt of your daughter's anger don't ask her directly about it. Start to become more interested in specifics about her life. Don't ask her how her day was. Instead ask her how she and her best friend are doing. If there is no response, do not push it. Let it go. Come back to the topic the next day or even a few days later. Next time bring up a different friend and a specific situation.

Don't try to force your daughter to talk if she is not receptive. Look instead for times when it is just the two of you and you can slip in some small talk and additional questions as well. It may be when you are shopping for clothes together, or driving to school in the car together. Also, try to weave messages into your daily routines. Reinforce your beliefs, values, and expectations on a daily basis through simple comments. Make these situations as informal as you can so your teenager doesn't think you are pumping her for information or shoving your opinions down her throat.

Competition and Jealousy

On the whole, society encourages competition. There is competition in social settings, in the workplace and even at home. We compete with our siblings for our parents' attention. As girls we compete with our mother for our father's attention, sometimes this can cause conflict. If a mother is not confident in her relationship with her husband, and the husband shows his love and attention toward his daughter and not to his wife, this can cause negative competition between the mother and daughter, especially if the wife is unable to express her feelings (which she may be unaware of) to her husband. Imagine the conflict this situation would create throughout your daughter's adolescent and teenage years.

In our family, competition was second nature. We were all involved in sports and our parents did an excellent job of showing us how competition could be healthy.

Competitiveness between siblings is part of us and encourages us to grow and be proud of each other, not jealous. But when competition is put into a negative context, it can divide families. This separation results in weakening ourselves and our family bonds because it is true that we are stronger in numbers. It feels good to be a part of something rather than being left out there on our own.

I like to think of healthy competition as what Bonnie Blair, the world-class female speed skater, said at a motivational talk, "I never competed with anyone except the clock." This drove her to create excellence in her speed skating career. She did so not by comparing herself to someone else, but by comparing her times and beating the clock. She was able to compete with herself which made her a world-class athlete and not a burned out athlete who could never keep up with her competitors.

In other words, it is important to look within yourself to see if your feeling of ill will toward someone like a husband, wife, or even a mentor is causing jealousy and creating competition with your daughter that results in unnecessary conflict.

The Fountain of Youth Gone Dry

Another potential problem with competition may occur if the mother has based all her self-esteem and self worth on her external appearance. As the years pass and she thinks or feels she is losing those assets which define herself, and her beautiful teenage daughter is blossoming, she may find herself competing for the attention of the young boys coming to pick up her daughter. It is possible the mom is trying to sustain her youth by wearing her daughter's clothes. One 15-year-old girl I interviewed confided in me that her mom tries to wear her clothes. When she confronts her about wearing clothes for her own age group the mother tells the daughter she is selfish because she won't share her clothing.

Remember that a daughter needs the mother to be an authority figure, she does not need her to be one of the girls. If this describes you as a parent, it is be very important to explore why you have these particular needs and feelings of competition with your daughter.

The Green-Eyed Monster

Jealousy can result from competition. During an episode on the *Oprah Winfrey Show* a mother revealed that she was jealous of her husband and her infant daughter's relationship. This was affecting their marriage. It turned out she was not able to have a good relationship with her father and when she witnessed how close her husband and daughter were becoming, her longing for a loving relationship with her own father was creating a huge rift in their family. That was an important realization for her to make

38

at this point in her life. There would have been a lot of unnecessary pain and suffering that would have occurred as her daughter grew into an adolescent and began exercising her independence had the mother not faced her unsettling past.

Parents can also be jealous of their daughter's opportunities. This can be very evident in the mother-daughter relationship if the mother has not come to grips with what she gave up to become a mother. A famous psychologist made a deeply philosophical statement when he said, "The most powerful influence on a child, is the unlived life of a parent." What he is trying to say is, if you are not comfortable with the choices you made and the consequences that came along with those choices, when you see your daughter having opportunities you never had, this will have a great influence on your child's life and possibly cause great conflict. Your unconscious jealousy will show up as anger and frustration toward your daughter and will even sometimes sabotage her ability to accomplish feats that you could never do. You may try to discourage her from trying something not out of concern for her safety, which it may seem like on the surface, but out of jealousy and anger about your past. As Debold, Wilson, and Malave put it, "daughters want to say, 'Mom get a life and you won't be so jealous of me.'"

The flip side of the statement "The most powerful influence on a child, is the unlived life of a parent," are the parents who never could accomplish a goal or dream of their own so they force it on their child. For example, the father who never made it past high school sports or was cut from the basketball team may put too much pressure on his daughter to compete if she has some interest in the sport. That is, instead of encouraging her with healthy unconditional support, the child feels pressure from the father to compete, which inevitably diminishes her enjoyment and willingness to participate in the sport.

In other words, take a good hard look at your past and see if maybe you want your daughter to be what YOU wanted to be, but didn't have the chance to be. Your daughter is a unique individual who may have some characteristics in common with you, but her goals and dreams may be very different from your own.

Incidentally, there is good pressure and bad pressure. Bad pressure is trying to fit your daughter, who is round, into a square hole. Pushing her to do something she really does not enjoy doing because you are getting something out of it is bad. Good pressure is encouraging your daughter to define her goals, her interests, and her dreams while helping her achieve them.

If you are not sure if your daughter is participating in something because she enjoys it or because she feels pressure from you, just ask her. Watch her body language as she replies because her verbal response may be very different from her non-verbal communication. Your daughter may say she is happy participating because she does not want to disappoint you, but her inability to look you in the eye or the shortness of the response and change of the subject may be giving you the real answer. Some communication experts say 60 percent of communication is non-verbal. Therefore, pay attention to her actions as well as her words. If her actions are inconsistent with what she is expressing verbally, you may have to explore a bit more.

Chapter Five

COPING WITH THE INEVITABLE

Dealing with your daughter (or the alien that is possessing your daughter's body for the time being) is not an easy task. Confrontations, disagreements, and heated discussions are inevitable, but they don't have to be commonplace or hurtful. It is important to realize that adolescence is difficult and challenging for you and your daughter. She is trying to establish who she is at this point in her life. And because this process for her is so unpredictable and frustrating it is essential that you develop some coping mechanisms for yourself in order for you to stay clearheaded the majority of the time so you can help your daughter through this tumultuous time.

You Are Not Perfect

An important thing to remember is that you are not going to do everything right all the time. Undoubtedly, as she reaches adolescence, your daughter will begin to notice that you are not perfect and she'll call you on it. This is a big change from your little girl thinking you have all the answers. She is changing rapidly through adolescence. The techniques that worked for the last eight to ten years unfortunately won't be very effective anymore. As I've said, confrontations are inevitable, but the following information will help you greatly reduce your pain and create a positive relationship with your daughter.

Don't Take It Personally

Easier said than done sometimes. But after a confrontation with your daughter it is important, for your own well-being, that you do not take it personally. The best thing you can

NOTE: Realizing parents aren't the all-knowing infallible human beings they once knew while growing up is actually a very healthy process. This shows girls that everyone makes mistakes and you cannot, and should not, expect perfection. This can also create conflict if the parent expects perfection from the child, and the child sees that their parents, who have so little tolerance for their mistakes, make mistakes themselves.

do for your daughter is to model appropriate behavior and conflict resolution skills. It is not easy, but in the heat of the battle you need to maintain your composure. If you don't, it is equally important to discuss with your daughter how you should have handled yourself in the situation. It will be very tempting, as some mothers I've interviewed have said, to tell your daughter how she should have handled the situation, but this approach will only push your daughter away more. She is tired and resistant to always hearing how you think she should have done something differently. You cannot control her behavior. You can only control yours. Influencing her behavior by modeling appropriate behavior is your goal.

Your daughter will not heed your advice if it is shoved down her throat. You must create an atmosphere where she feels comfortable asking you for advice. She may surprise you and come up with her own solutions. Impossible? Read the section on Empathic Listening in the next chapter for ideas.

When your daughter's actions hurt your feelings, do not take it personally. If she is being disrespectful, this needs to be addressed, but if instead of talking to you when she comes home from school, your daughter closes her door and talks on the phone with her friends, do not be hurt or offended. Instead, try this exercise: First, try to think of a reason why your daughter may be acting this way. Then, think of any other possible reasons she may be acting this way. And finally, give her the benefit of the doubt. Convince yourself that your daughter was acting this way not to hurt your feelings deliberately, but for any number of reasons, which may not have anything to do with you.

Just remember, your daughter needs you in a very different way than she did only a few short years ago. Therefore, do not take your confrontations personally so that you become angry or hurt and subsequently withdraw from her. She needs you now more than ever.

Talk to Your Parents

If it is possible, talking with your mom and dad about your teenage and adolescent years may be a real eye-opener. If you had more difficulty with your mom, her recollections might be a bit more difficult to hear. It was for me. Listening to these perceptions of how you acted toward her when you were a teen may shed some light on how your daughter is acting. Are you experiencing similar situations or feelings that your mom or dad experienced with you? You may not remember these situations, but your parents probably do.

Speaking to your mom and dad about those trying years may help you remember what you were going through, but even more importantly, it may help you understand what your parents went through. It may help you see your parents as real people. As Dr. Harriet Lerner, author of *The Mother Dance* explains in regards to mothers and daughters, "Knowing our mothers as real people helps us to know ourselves better. It also makes it less likely that we will mindlessly follow or rebel against family patterns."

42

Getting in Touch with Your Past

In the last chapter, you were asked to see if you could identify with any of the sources listed. This process involved really looking at yourself and your behavior and seeing if it may be affecting your relationship with your daughter.

If your relationship with your mom or dad was difficult, don't dwell on it. That is not the purpose here. Instead, acknowledge the fact that because you and one or both of your parents had tough times, this does not determine how you parent your daughter, unless you let it. By accepting these difficult relationships it allows you to learn from your past and move on. As Dr. Phil McGraw, author of *Life Strategies* and frequent guest on the *Oprah Winfrey Show* writes, "You can't change what you don't acknowledge."

In other words, if you don't recognize the negative patterns you were exposed to and allow your children to be exposed to the same negative patterns, then you are the one to blame for passing them on to your children. You cannot blame Mom or Dad anymore. You are an adult and every day you have the ability to make choices. You are in control of your life. If you continue to pass on the negative parenting that you received, you are doing a great disservice to your children and to your community.

If you are having difficulty relating to any of the situations listed in the last chapter it may be that you are having difficulty getting back in touch with feelings and thoughts you had during your adolescent and teenage years. In addition, if attempting to remember your past is drumming up a significant amount of pain, please seek out the aid of a therapist to help you deal with your past. Don't avoid getting in touch with your past, but don't go it alone if it is too painful to remember.

One path you can take to help you remember what it was like to be a teenager is to get out some old pictures from that time in your life and start to look through the photos. You can even use old notes or letters from classmates as well as yearbooks from that era. Ask your parents if they have any of your old notebooks or report cards. If you want to get really creative, you can make a collage of all these old memories to make this process more fun. Call up an old friend from way back and talk to her about the times in your life that you shared. She may be able to shake out the cobwebs and aid you in realizing something about your goals and dreams that you revealed to her a long time ago.

All these items and conversations will drum up memories from the past and help you identify the thoughts and feelings you had during that time. Take an hour or two to do this exercise. I know you are thinking, who has an hour or two to do this? Well, you don't have to do this all at once and, remember, if you continue to do what you've always done, then you'll continue to get what you've always got.

As you are doing this exercise, ask yourself these questions:

1) How is my life different today than what I thought it would be? Is it different by my own choice or did certain circumstances or people make it different?

2) Did I have the support of my parents in my decision making? Whether the answer is yes or no, how did that make me feel? And what resulted from their support or lack thereof?

3) Did my parents listen to me and encourage me to achieve my own goals? Whether yes or no, how did that make me feel? And what resulted from their actions?

4) If you are a mom now, how was your relationship with your mom?
   If you are a dad, did you have any sisters that you observed while growing up? If so, what was their relationship like with your mom? Call them up and ask if you don't recall.
   If you are a dad and don't have any sisters, then ask your wife or female friends what their relationship with their mom was when they were an adolescent and/or teenager. (You may need to ask them to do the exercise with you so they can get in touch with their feelings about the past.)

5) In what ways did I value myself years ago? Was it my looks, my grades, or my friend-ships? And do I still value myself today by those same standards?

6) Lastly, how would I rate my own self-esteem? (High, Okay, or Low)
   How do I convey this to my daughter?
   Ask the people around you if you consistently make negative comments about yourself.

Now that you have answered some of these questions, you are prepared to start listening to your daughter. Just hearing her does not count, really listening to understand is what matters.

Talk to Other Parents

If nothing else, talking to other parents about their daughters will enable you to realize the fact that you are not a horrible parent. Other parents are dealing with similar situations with their daughters. There is definitely something to be said for knowing that others may be faced with the same dilemmas with their daughters. The least this will accomplish is that it proves you are not crazy. It is not your imagination, and you are not a horrible parent. I could almost guarantee that almost every parent who has either raised a teenage girl or who is presently raising a teenage girl would have some story to share with you. All you have to do is ask.

How can you find out what other parents are dealing with? If your daughter is involved in any extracurricular activities where parents have an opportunity to meet each other, simply ask a mom or dad if they have noticed a change in their daughter's attitude since she has reached adolescence and high school. Be ready for an earful.

If you do not have any of those opportunities, keep your eyes open for workshops or special events dealing with this issue. Often churches, and even hospital wellness programs, will offer roundtable discussions and workshops.

And finally, if you are dealing with a situation that you feel would be too difficult to change on your own, seek out advice from a counselor who works with teens and adolescents. Look in your yellow pages under "Teen Help Services." There may be a number you can call to obtain advice.

Mentors

Mentors can be extremely useful to a teenager. Positive female role models are especially important at this time in your daughter's life. As we have discussed in the chapter on self-esteem, a girl's self-esteem plummets as she goes through adolescence and into high school. Mentors or trusted counselors can assist your daughter in dealing with the topics that are difficult for her to talk to her parents about. An effective mentor will encourage your daughter to open the lines of communication with her parents. A mentor can be an adult female friend of the family, a coach, a teacher, or a guidance counselor at school.

I have been most effective at mentoring high school girls after I have established a rapport with them. Basically, I listen to them. By listening to what their feelings are and not judging them, I establish a trusting relationship. Parents have come to me and asked, "How do you get through to these kids? I can tell my daughter the same things that you do, but she doesn't believe me until she hears it from you." I believe part of that is due to the teenager not being exposed to my flaws like they are at home with their parents. One mom put it, "My daughter just loves to see me mess up or make a mistake. It almost seems like she enjoys it sometimes." At this turbulent time in her life, an adolescent girl will notice your imperfections (and point them out to you) as another way of establishing her own identity. Proving once again to you and to herself that she is her own person.

Mentors may be more effective relaying the positive messages you are trying to communicate to your child because the longing to be different doesn't exist between mentor and student. You can assure these positive messages are being exchanged by meeting the mentor if you don't already know her. If the situation presents itself and your daughter is not within earshot, first thank your child's mentor for being there for your daughter. Then let her know you are available if there is anything she would like to discuss with you.

45

In addition, if your daughter appears to have a mentor that she can relate to or if one of your close friends appears to strike a chord with your daughter, do not allow your jealousy to sabotage their relationship. If you are feeling jealous over your daughter's relationship with another female adult (and the adult seems to have had a positive impact on your child) encourage the friendship. Feelings of jealousy may result from your own insecurity about your relationship. As one mother of three daughters put it "my relationship changed a great deal when my daughter became a teenager. It's like you are losing them for awhile, but they will be back".

Are you sure how to connect your daughter with a mentor? She may not have the opportunity to meet adults who have the time to mentor her. If that is the case, there are many mentoring programs offered in cities all over the United States. Many times there is no fee to the families, and the mentors are paid through publicly and privately funded agencies. Big Brothers and Big Sisters is one of the most common programs, but with a little effort, you will probably find other programs in your area or someone at your daughter's school to whom she relates well.

*Note: If you feel that an adult mentor is having a negative impact on your daughter, it is definitely a good idea to approach the person and/or the agency who employs the mentor. Simply sharing your feelings with them may clear up the situation right away. It may be a misunderstanding, but as a parent you have the right to investigate the situation. You cannot rely on a mentor to take your place. Her role should be that of a positive adult influence on your daughter, not as a parental replacement.

Chapter Six

INFLUENCING YOUR DAUGHTER'S BEHAVIOR

Let's face it, adolescence and teenage years are tough. We may remember some of the problems we had growing up but now there are more stresses on children than ever before. Ninety-five percent of the teens I interviewed told me that they felt very stressed out or depressed at times. Over 50 percent have confided in me that they have thought about suicide. Parents, you may look at the situation your daughter is stressed about and think, "That's no big deal, it'll pass." But from your daughter's frame of reference it IS a big deal and no matter how many times you tell her you went through the same things and it'll pass, it still is a significant stress to her at that point in her life. Telling her, "Don't be silly, you're making a mountain out of a mole hill," or "It's just a phase you are going through," will not help her situation. As a matter of fact, it will severely hinder your attempts at communicating with your daughter.

For those of you who want a quick fix or some magic potion to change your daughter's behavior, it's just not going to happen. The reason is, you can't change her. She is an individual, unique in all aspects. She is not you reincarnated. Yet, most often parents try to relate to their children through *their own* frame of reference. The only way you can understand your daughter's behavior is by relating to her through *her* frame of reference. The only way you can influence your daughter's behavior is by changing your own.

The following poem by an Anglican bishop illustrates this point.

> *When I was young and free and my imagination had no limits,*
> *I dreamed of changing the world;*
>
> *As I grew older and wiser I realized the world would not change.*
>
> *And I decided to shorten my sights somewhat and change only my country.*
> *But it seemed too immovable.*
>
> *As I entered my twilight years, in one last desperate attempt,*
> *I sought to change my family, those closest to me,*
> *but alas they would have none of it.*

47

And now here I lie on my deathbed and realize
(perhaps for the first time)
that if only I'd changed myself first, then by
example I may have influenced my family
and with their encouragement and support
I may have bettered my country, and who knows
I may have changed the world.

Modeling the appropriate behavior yourself is a very effective way to influence your daughter. When this is accomplished, your daughter will be less defensive and communicate more honestly and more often with you. Remember, it is never too late to change.

Modeling Behavior

When your daughter was born, you were the first source of information. When she couldn't speak, she would mimic your movements. When she began to speak, she would mimic your movements and your words. You were setting an example for your child to learn from virtually the moment she was born.

Most of this learning is embedded in the subconscious, usually from repetitive exposure to words or actions. This explains why all of a sudden we open our mouths and something that our mom or dad used to say comes flying out. Many times it is something we swore we would never say when we were parents. Children learn more from what you do than what you say.

During adolescence, as much as she tries to avoid you and does not want you to be around, your child will model your behaviors. She may act as though you do not exist or that you know nothing. This may make you feel that she does not want you or need you anymore. On the contrary, over 90 percent of the teens I surveyed said it was very important to have a good relationship with their parents. Your daughter needs you now more than ever. It is very important that you continue to make an effort to model appropriate behaviors for your daughter throughout her teenage years. Some examples from teens include: "My mom always expects us to be on time. She gets angry when we are late. But when she is supposed to pick us up from somewhere she is always late." Another teen states, "My mom gets so mad at me when I talk to my friends on the phone. I admit, sometimes I can talk to them for hours but so does she. Sometimes she'll be on the phone with her friends for more than an hour but for some reason it's not okay for me." Another teen talks about her dad, "He always expects me to be polite and respectful toward his friends when they are on the phone or when they come over. But when my friends call he is so rude. He hardly talks to them. When they stop over, he rarely even says Hello." And another teen, "Whenever my friends and I are talking about someone at our school, my parents always tell us not to talk behind their back. But at the dinner table my parents are always making fun of somebody at work or someone they have just talked to or seen."

These are examples of the old, "do as I say, not as I do" clichè. It may work when your daughter is young, but when she reaches her adolescence or teen years, it may be the source of unnecessary conflict. When I spoke to one father about this he said, "It is always easy to tell your kids what to do without ever thinking about what you are doing yourself. When they bring it up to you, it seems as though they are being a smart-aleck but really, they have a point."

In other words, if you want a certain behavior from your daughter, you must model it. They may not admit it to you, but they still do need you. Remember, they need you now more than ever.

The catch is your daughter's needs are not the same as when she was zero to ten years old. Therefore, you cannot treat her the same way. Your little girl is somewhere between child and adult. Where she is on this continuum can change in a matter of minutes. She no longer feels comfortable being a little girl, but she knows she is not quite a woman yet. What a confusing time this is for her.

Confusing for her. Yes. Stressful for you? Definitely.

Next we will discuss how learning to deal with your own stress may help influence your daughter's behavior and avoid some unnecessary confrontations.

Dealing with Your Own Stress

Before we move on to how to be an effective listener in the next section, it is important to increase some awareness about yourself and your behaviors. By this I mean, it is essential to recognize the physiological signs your body gives off before you are just about to blow up or retreat from a situation. It's relatively impossible to listen if steam is shooting from your ears.

During your stress-induced fit of rage or period of withdrawal, your daughter does not rationalize that stress is the reason you are acting this way. Instead, she perceives the anger or apathy as a reflection on her. In other words, if you react to your own stresses by directing anger toward your daughter or by ignoring her, she will think you are angry at her (which may or may not be true) or that you just don't care if you fail to react at all.

Let's face it. As I stated, there is not going to be much listening going on if you can't control your emotions (usually anger) or if your daughter's perception is that you can't control your emotions. Have you ever heard, "Why should I tell you? You'll just get mad."

Sound familiar? Let me explain. It is my belief that some of the unnecessary conflict that arises between you and your daughter may certainly be a result of the sources of conflict we discussed in chapter 4. But let's face it, every argument you have with your daughter is not based on whether or not you have achieved what you wanted in life. Rather, stress plays an essential role in arguments in any relationship. The way you react to stressful situations will help or hinder your ability to communicate with your daughter. I don't think that I have to convince you that everyone in today's world of stock market swings and road rage is experiencing a significant amount of stress.

First, let's define stress. Webster states, "stress is a factor that produces bodily or mental tension." So picture this, you just came home from work. Traffic was horrible. You arrived late and it was your turn to cook dinner. Your daughter is talking on the phone and has been home for at least an hour. You lay into her about how irresponsible it was for her to be at home, knowing that you were late and she did not even start dinner. Now, because of her being irresponsible, the whole family is starving.

This particular reaction is based on two stresses, the horrible traffic and you arriving home late. That situation really didn't improve your relationship with your teenage daughter at all. Now let's also add that your daughter had a horrible day, too. She just found out that her best friend was talking about her behind her back. So her response to your anger is that you don't understand what she is going through and everything is always her fault, and on and on while she stomps off to her room.

Here's another situation. Let's say you have been home all day with the younger children in your home. It is the end of the day. You are beat. The kids are hungry. The repairman never showed up. You are supposed to be meeting some friends in an hour but your spouse is late getting home and hasn't called. Your daughter walks in and tells you she needs her volleyball uniform for tonight's game and cannot believe you have not washed it yet. Needless to say, all hell breaks loose and you start yelling at your daughter about how hard you work and she does not appreciate anything. She is spoiled and has no consideration for others. After mudslinging back and forth for a bit your daughter runs out of the room crying and slams her bedroom door.

These situations could not fit Webster's definition more perfectly. What could you have done? What were some of the warning signs you exhibited before you blew up? Fatigue is a common factor in escalating a stressful situation. So, if you are fatigued, be aware of this and take some precautions so you don't lose it.

First you must understand the three components of the stress cycle:
1) Perception - your interpretation
2) Emotion - usually anger or fear

3) Fight or Flight - an autonomic (as well as automatic) response to physiologically help you deal with the stressful situation

Of these three, let's look at the emotional aspect first. In a stressful situation, the underlying emotion is usually anger or fear. In the first example you are probably experiencing both anger and fear as you are driving home, dealing with horrible traffic (anger) and knowing you are going to be late (fear and/or anger). When you arrive at home you see your daughter and your perception is that she was just sitting around the whole time while everyone is starving and doing nothing to help you (more anger). So you immediately blow your top or make a sarcastic comment to her because of your stress level. This incidentally was your fight or flight mechanism. Guess what? You chose to fight.

Your daughter in turn, who is stressed herself, probably due to fear of losing her best friend (and always getting blamed for everything), blows up and stomps off to her room. She chose flight. Do you feel better after yelling at her? Probably not. You either feel guilty that you lost it or angry that she was disrespectful toward you.

Your perception of the situation was that she was being irresponsible and that she should have known you wanted her to start dinner if you were going to be late. Your daughter's perception is that you don't care about her. She is thinking, "You were the one who is late, not me."

The anger that you feel toward your daughter is displaced. Deep down you are really angry at yourself and possibly fear that you are not a good mother or father because you have not gotten dinner on the table. Your daughter is the easy target and you take it out on her.

Let's look at the second example. You have been home all day and are tired. (Red flag!!) When your daughter walks in and demands her uniform and tells you she cannot believe it is not washed you are feeling both anger and fear. You are angry that she is so inconsiderate and is only thinking of yourself. But underneath that anger you are probably feeling guilty or fearful that in fact you are a bad mom because you did not get to wash the uniform. This may sound ridiculous, but if you really sit down and think about it there is more than likely some truth to that statement. Usually there is a subconscious fear hidden under anger.

So, you both begin to yell at each other (fight) and your daughter leaves the room (flight). You may even feel a bit of relief when the situation is over because you have gotten rid of some frustration. But more often than not you will feel badly about the situation or remain angry with your daughter. Undoubtedly, this conflict will cause additional stress in your relationship with your daughter.

Your perception is that she is ungrateful and thinks you have nothing to do but take care of her. Your daughter's perception is that mom is psycho and that you do not love her or care about her.

Now, let us look at the situations and see how you could have handled it better. Remember, we are looking at you because you can't change your daughter, you can only change yourself and how you react. By making yourself aware of the signs your body gives you that are leading up to a fight or flight response you can gain the ability to maintain control in situations where you may have otherwise "lost it."

For example, right before I explode or reach my limit, I start to breathe much shallower. I feel myself sweating and tensing up. Then if I don't catch myself, I am a raving lunatic and lose any credibility I may have had with the people I am directing my anger toward. Shallow breathing and sweating are my signals that I am about to lose it if I don't change this pattern. Do you know your signals? The next time you are in a stressful situation, try to notice what you are feeling before it goes too far.

Some people start to cry in stressful situations. This could be avoided by concentrating on deep breathing before you've reached the point of crying. I believe that concentrating on your breathing—using diaphragmatic breathing—will help you gain control and keep you more relaxed. Slowing your breathing lowers your heart rate and keeps the muscles from tensing up. (Refer to the boxed section on diaphragmatic breathing for information on how to master it.)

Do not forget about the fatigue factor. If you have had a rough day and are very fatigued, remind yourself that you will be more apt to have a short fuse. Reminding yourself of this and being aware of the signs that lead up to the blow up will help you stay in control in stressful situations.

How could you have handled these situations differently?

First situation: You are driving home. You are feeling very tense because of traffic. Right now try some breathing exercises or keep a tape or CD of some mellow music in the car. Don't fall asleep listening to the music! The point is to release some of the tension that is being caused by the external environment.

A technique to help road rage or anger in your car that I use is when someone cuts me off, instead of thinking #*@!#* you!, I try to think or say "Bless you." Even if I say it with anger, it doesn't seem to effect me as much as if I used a certain gesture or certain four-letter word to get my point across. You see, if you allow yourself to get angry and stressed, the person who has cut you off has won. You are wasting too much energy on him or her. You allow that person to stay with you and effect your mind, your body and your life when in the grand scheme of things, it is not really a big deal. Some people have told me that it actually makes them feel better when they blow off a little steam at someone who they don't know and will never see again. I think, however, that it's just a waste of time and energy.

To drive this point home, let me tell you is a story about two monks walking along a creek. One was an older monk and the other was relatively young. The order that these monks belonged to did not allow them to touch women. This was considered sinful. As they were walking along the creek they saw a woman standing on their side of the creek. On the other side of the creek was a small child crying out to his mother to come across because that was the way home. As the monks approached the woman they noticed that she had a cane and seemed physically unable to cross the creek to get to her child and continue her journey home. So when the two monks reached the woman the younger monk just kept on walking by, ignoring the situation. The older monk stopped, picked up the woman, and walked her across the creek to the other side where she could continue her journey home. Neither monk said anything, but it was obvious the younger monk was very agitated and bothered by the fact that his friend had not only touched this woman but carried her to the other side of the creek. Finally after an hour, he couldn't stand it anymore and he burst out and said, "I cannot believe you broke the sacred rule and carried that woman across the creek." The older monk turned to him and said, "I simply carried her across the creek, you have carried her with you for over an hour." The monks walked in silence once again.

You arrive home late probably still feeling tired but less stressed. You realize dinner is late and you see your daughter sitting in the kitchen on the phone. She seems upset. This is something that you would not have noticed before because you yourself were so angry and stressed.

You ask your daughter to please get off the phone and help you with dinner because you are already off to a late start. Your daughter makes a snide remark and gets off the phone in a huff. You feel your stress signals again—shallow breathing, red in the face. You begin to breathe deeply and explain to your daughter that you can see something is bothering her, but right now you feel badly because you are late and there is no dinner on the table for the family. If she could just help you right now you would really appreciate it. Probably under protest your daughter will help you. But this is an opportunity to let her know you care about her by asking her about something nonchalantly while the two of you are getting dinner ready. If you would happen to ask about her best friend, Susie, you would have hit the nail on the head and your daughter may open up to you at that time. If she does not, at least she gets the feeling that you care. If she doesn't open up, do not push it. You may want to try other techniques we discuss in this chapter.

By being aware of your stress signals and consciously making an effort to not let these meaningless external situations get to you, you have avoided a major conflict and many hurt feelings, including your own.

Sound simple? Well really it is. The hard part is getting into the habit of consistently being consciously aware of your stress signals. It may take a while to get the hang of this technique, but keep trying. It is worth the effort.

Granted, there will still be times that you may "lose it." After all, we are human. The best approach after you have blown your top for no reason or because you were angry about an unrelated situation is to apologize. Done sparingly, this can be very effective. Your daughter will undoubtedly accept your apology (unless this is the 100th time you have apologized in a month) and she will learn that nobody's perfect and you do value her feelings. Your daughter will then see you as a human being that can make mistakes and admit to them. Seeing you as a real person, not someone who always seems to know everything, helps your daughter to know herself better. When you apologize for inappropriate behavior you not only show your daughter you value her feelings, but you eliminate the unnecessary power struggle that causes so many problems between teenage girls and their parents. Again, done sparingly, modeling this behavior will have a very positive effect on your daughter. She will surely respect you more and understand the importance of owning up to her own mistakes.

When you apologize, take time to explain why you blew up and how you could have handled the situation better. But also make her realize that she is accountable for her actions as well. Ask her what she should have done differently to avoid this difficult situation in the future. This would be a great learning experience for her.

What is diaphragmatic breathing? The diaphragm is a muscle directly beneath your rib cage that helps control your breathing. As infants, we automatically breathe from our diaphragm, which is much more efficient. Relaxation and meditation techniques utilize diaphragmatic breathing to become centered and relaxed. As adults, most of us breathe much less efficiently using the muscles in our chest. Breathing from the upper chest inhibits us from utilizing our lung capacity and wastes energy by using accessory muscles to breathe.

Let's do an exercise.

Lie down on your back and place your right hand on your stomach just below the rib cage and your left hand on your upper chest. Now, as you take a deep breath in, see if you feel your shoulders rising, or your stomach rising under your hand. If you don't feel your stomach rising then you are using your accessory breathing muscles in your chest versus the more efficient diaphragm. Breathing from your diaphragm may take practice but it can be mastered.

Why is diaphragmatic breathing important? It is a more efficient way of breathing and can help you stay centered at times when you feel you may have a tendency to lose control. Try it. The next time a co-worker or your child starts to irritate you, try breathing deeply and use your diaphragm. You will notice that you do not become stressed as quickly or easily. Physiologically, your blood pressure will stay at a normal reading and your pulse will be stable or possibly even lower. Diaphragmatic breathing will enable you to reverse or avoid those initial signs of losing control. You will be more apt to make rational statements and control yourself in stressful situations.

Now that you are calm, cool, and collected, you are ready to listen. The following technique on empathic listening will undoubtedly improve your relationship with your daughter.

The Art of Listening

This is probably one of the MOST IMPORTANT areas in this book. And it will definitely be the most challenging. This is not a difficult concept to understand, but it will be challenging for you to change some ways that you have communicated all of your life. The reward for accepting this challenge is that you will allow your daughter to problem-solve for herself and at the same time she will become more receptive to your advice.

If you are not willing to change your listening style then ask yourself these questions. Is what you are doing now working? Are you getting the results you want in all the relationships in your life? If not, read on because if you apply this listening technique, you will be amazed at the results with every relationship in your life, not just the relationship between you and your daughter.

Empathic Listening

You may have heard this term before. Besides the fact that I have referred to empathic listening several times in preceding chapters, Stephen Covey, the author of *Seven Habits for Highly Successful People* and *Seven Habits for Highly Effective Families* mentions empathic listening in his books. Mr. Covey describes this technique as, "seek first to understand and then to be understood."

The importance of understanding first was illustrated to me when I attended a one-hour discussion group on dealing with adolescent girls. Adults, both male, and female, mostly attended the discussion. Also present were four or five adolescent girls. Parents were raising questions of how they can get their daughters to listen to what they wanted to say and to allow them to help their daughters with their problems. After hearing these questions from parents I turned to the girls and asked, "What's more important to you, to be understood, or to have someone tell you how you can solve your problems?" Each of the girls I asked answered, "It's more important that our parents understand."

Instead of listening, most of us seek to be understood first because we want to get our point across. We waste so much energy trying to prove we are right. Some of us never seek to understand! Many spend their lifetimes trying only to get their own point across to prove they are "right." Just turn on talk shows during the day and watch the guests relate to each other. This is a great example of how some types of communication can be totally ineffective.

A benefit of empathic listening is giving your daughter the feeling that you really do know what she is going through, that you are not just being critical or judgmental. As Deborah Phillips, author of *How to Give Your Child A Great Self-Image* puts it, "Empathy... is a way of expressing love that will have a direct impact on your child's self-image. By empathizing, you are sending your child a clear-cut message that she's an important, worthwhile, and valuable person."

You will notice that once she feels you value her feelings, she will be more receptive to your advice. Another observation that you will make by listening empathically is she will come up with her own answers to problems because this technique helps her find the answer from within. In addition, more often than not, the answer to the problem that your daughter comes up with will probably be as good or better than the advice you would have given her.

Empathic listening also gives your daughter control. This issue can be very important during adolescence and teenage years. Loss of control over her own life can have detrimental effects on your daughter which could result in depression, eating disorders, alcohol and drug abuse or teenage pregnancy.

By trying to understand first, you can become vulnerable. Once you become vulnerable, you open yourself up to be influenced. At the same time, you do not have to agree with what the other person is saying to show you understand them.

Not convinced that this is an important technique? Let me share with you the conversation I had with one teenage girl. "When my mom and I get into an argument it's usually because she is not listening to what I am trying to say. Then the argument gets worse and whatever she wants me to do, I'll do the opposite. Or if she says I'm lazy then I'll be lazy because I know that drives her crazy."

After I interviewed this last teen I recalled a short poem I saw on a bulletin board where I worked which really drove home what she was saying.

PLEASE LISTEN
When I ask you to listen to me
And you start giving me advice,
You have not done what I asked.
When I ask you to listen to me
and you begin to tell me why
I shouldn't feel that way,
You are trampling on my feelings.
When I ask you to listen to me
and you feel you have to do something
to solve my problem, you have failed me,
strange as that may seem.
Listen! All I ask is that you listen.
Don't talk or do, just hear me.

Use empathic listening and you will see the change in your daughter's actions, sometimes without even having to tell her what you want.

First we will discuss how to master this listening technique and then I will give examples of how to use this technique with your daughter.

There are two components to empathic listening:
1) Paraphrasing
2) Validating with a feeling reflection

Paraphrasing means that after listening to what your daughter says, repeat it back to her but not in the same words. For example, if your daughter says, "Dad, I really want to go to Janice's party next weekend," instead of simply replying "no," you could say, "So, it seems like you are very excited about going to Janice's next weekend." You are just repeating back to her what she was saying in your own words. This technique will allow you to get your daughter to start talking.

In addition to paraphrasing you must include a validation of what she is feeling. Here is a conversation that you might run across at home. First, I'll give you an example of not listening effectively. Then we'll go through the same situation utilizing the empathic listening technique.

Daughter:	"Mom, I really hate my English teacher."
Mom:	"Now honey, why would you say something like that?"
Daughter:	"Because he's a jerk!"
Mom:	"Well, why is he a jerk?"
Daughter	"I don't know. He just is!"
Mom:	"Okay, give me a reason why you think he's a jerk."

Daughter: "Well, he gave me a C on my last paper. Can you believe it?"
Mom: "You know, if you wouldn't spend so much time on the telephone and put some effort into your homework then you wouldn't be getting Cs on your paper."
Daughter: "Whatever! (Rolls her eyes and stomps out of the room)

More than likely, the daughter was trying to tell her mom something about that teacher but felt her mom didn't understand, so the daughter shut her mom out.

This is the empathic listening method:

Daughter: "Geez, I really hate my English teacher."
Mom/Dad   "It sounds like you are really angry with your English teacher" (paraphrasing/ validating feeling of anger)
Daughter: "Well yeah, I am. He gave me a stupid C on my paper."
Mom/Dad: "So your teacher gave you a C on your paper. Is that why you are upset?" (Paraphrasing/validating feeling)
Daughter: "Well, it's not just that, I mean I probably deserved a C because I didn't put much time into it. But it's his fault cuz that's not the only reason I hate him."
Mom/Dad   "So the C isn't what is really upsetting you?" (Paraphrasing)
Daughter: "No, I just don't like the rude comments he makes to the girls in the class."

Now you are getting somewhere. Most parents, if they expect better than a C, would have reacted in a manner similar to the first example. But in the second case, the daughter felt understood enough to tell her mother or father what was really bothering her. Now they have uncovered the real issue and can work that out together. You may or may not want to discuss the C on the paper later!

Another thing to consider is your body language as you are communicating with your daughter. Communication experts estimate that 10 percent of communication is conveyed by words, 30 percent by voice, and 60 percent by body, or nonverbal communication. Therefore, while listening to your daughter you want her to know that she has your full attention or she will sense by your body language that you really don't care or understand. In other words, if you are too tired or don't have time, you may have to fake it and use attentive body language like making direct eye contact, stopping what you are doing, and sitting attentively. Another alternative, if you are unable to give your daughter your full attention, is to schedule a time in the next 24 hours when you can sit down and talk with her. Explain to her that you are truly interested in her feelings, but this is not a good time for you. You better make sure to keep that appointment or you lose all your credibility.

One of the biggest criticisms of empathic listening is that it takes too much time. This is certainly true at the beginning of this process. Once mastered, though, your daughter will feel more comfortable getting to the point because she knows you will make the effort to understand. And in the long run, it will take far less of your time and energy to deal with issues because your daughter will come up with the answers herself.

In addition, becoming an effective listener in your child's eyes may allow her to feel comfortable approaching you on serious issues and hopefully prevent negative outcomes that would have taken up much more of your time and energy than simply learning how to listen effectively.

Communicate with Your Daughter

You may be thinking, "That listening stuff is great, but I can't even get my daughter to talk to me. I can't really practice listening if she isn't talking." One teenager that I spoke to who had written on her survey that her mother really bugged her and they really didn't talk much told me that her mother tried too hard. (Boy, it seems like you're damned if you do and you're damned if you don't.) Every day, when she came home from school, her mom would ask her twenty questions. Incidentally, for teenagers, the worst time to try and strike up a conversation is right when they get home from school. These questions may have seemed to be unintrusive questions to start up a conversation but it was to the point that "How are you" was annoying her daughter and neither the mom nor the daughter knew why.

In cases like these, when the teen or adolescent just won't open up or anything the parent says gets a sarcastic response, there probably was poor communication in the past that lead to this situation. Another reason could be that the daughter just needs her privacy and wants to be left alone. This is very common for teens when they arrive home from school. They probably just need to unwind a bit from a hectic day.

In the case where nothing seems to work, if you are truly willing to attempt to seek first to understand her and try empathic listening, write her a letter. This is a very common form of communication used by teens and adolescents to communicate their feelings. This form of communication is familiar to them and by doing this you are, in a sense, entering their world. All the letter simply has to state is that you know the two of you haven't been getting along lately and you would like to schedule a time to talk or go for an ice cream or to a movie because your relationship is very important. In addition you can explain that you truly are going to make an effort to listen to her and try to understand where she is coming from.

Don't expect an answer right away. Give it a day or two to sink in and maybe then approach her if she hasn't already approached you. When you do approach her, don't go into a long monologue about how you spent your time writing the letter and it's rude not to respond. Just simply ask if you can schedule a time where you can sit down and talk. More than likely, she will say okay and you've got your chance. If she doesn't respond favorably and doesn't display any of the signs of a more serious problem (this will be discussed in the chapter

7) then you may want to write her another letter to explain what you are trying accomplish. Tell her that you feel you have done a poor job of listening to her and you want to start over. After she gets back into to the chair that she just fell out of while reading your letter, your daughter will undoubtedly give you a chance because you implied that you are partly to blame for the communication problem.

When you finally have her attention, start out by telling her you would like to put the past behind you and let her know you want to start over. Don't tell her that you are ultimately trying to get her to change her behavior. That won't go over very well. Tell her that you are going to change your listening style and you hope she will give you a chance. Children will always give their parents another chance especially if asked sincerely. A big no-no would be to start delving right into her life and all her problems. Have patience. If she opens up, fine. But don't pry!

It may take a few attempts to get used to the fact that even though you may want to, you can't just start giving your advice or opinions right away without first trying to understand where she is coming from. A few good suggestions from moms that I spoke to are:

1) Set ground rules. Some fights and disagreements are inevitable so set ground rules in advance. For example, if your daughter feels that you are starting to climb back on that soap box, have her do something to signal to you so you know you are losing her. It could be clearing her throat, signalling for a time out, or just saying "You are doing it again." Let her know that you will not tolerate her rolling her eyes, interrupting, name calling, or other signs of disrespect. This also holds true for the parent. If you want a certain behavior from your daughter, you must model it yourself.

2) Don't beat yourself up. You are doing the best you can.

3) Don't stop trying. If your daughter gets frustrated with you, explain to her (maybe in a letter) that it takes time and you are giving it your best effort.

4) If you were wrong, it is okay to admit it.

5) Have realistic expectations. Start out slowly. Things will not change overnight. Your daughter may not confide her deepest thoughts and feelings to you. Over 70 percent of the girls surveyed stated they did not share their deepest thoughts and feelings with their parents because often times, they aren't sure themselves what their deepest thoughts and feelings are at that time. But as your relationship grows you may help your daughter get in touch with her deepest thoughts and desires by giving her the control to develop them and encouraging her to explore those feelings.

6) Remember, you cannot change your daughter no matter how hard you try. You can only control your actions.

7) Don't take it personally. If your daughter does not want to spend as much time with you or if she shuts her bedroom door to talk on the phone with her friends, don't take it personally. As one mom told me, "She'll be back. It just might take awhile." If you try to force yourself on her because you long for that closeness, it will push her further away. Simple occasional reminders will let her know you will be there when she needs you.

> NOTE: The empathic listening technique can also work with disciplining. In other words, you may understand how she feels but still don't agree with her. And though she may be angry that you won't let her go to the party on a school night, she will at least know that you are attempting to understand where she is coming from. You must continue to be parents and set boundaries for your daughter. Remember, your daughter doesn't need you to be her pal, she needs you to be an authority when necessary.

Enter Her World

Another technique that parents I surveyed found to be effective was to enter their daughter's world. Now, there is a definite line between hanging out with your daughter and her friends as if you were back in your adolescence and entering her world on her terms. A few suggestions would be to go see a movie together that she wants to see or watch a television show that she enjoys watching. After seeing the movie, talk about it and ask her questions to show her that you value her input. If your daughter has hobbies, ask her to show you some things as if she were the teacher.

All of these suggestions help your daughter to realize that you respect and validate her as a human. You are not trying to run her life completely, but instead you are willing to learn from her and listen to her thoughts and feelings. Even though you may disagree on various topics, you are demonstrating that you respect her. You don't expect her to be you reincarnated. Imagine how you would feel if more people allowed you to be who you are versus who they want you to be.

Role Playing

This technique works especially well with younger children in their early adolescence. Older teens may think you are crazy, but if you can get them to sit with you for a minute, role playing can be extremely beneficial.

Why? Most adolescents and teens are experiencing almost everything for the first time. They do not have prior life experience to handle the difficult situations they may face. Our adolescents and teens today are being exposed to drugs and alcohol much earlier. Our girls are being pressured into having sex or becoming intimate at a much younger age than five or ten years ago. If you role play with your children this gives them an opportunity to practice what they would do or say if they were faced with a difficult situation.

Sitting down and making up certain scenarios can be fun and enjoyable for you and your daughter. It can bring you closer. Chances are, she might be able to teach you a few things about what is going on at her school. You may feel uncomfortable at first but if it helps your daughter resist the temptation of drugs, alcohol, or pressured sex, is it not worth feeling a little bit uncomfortable?

Chapter Seven

When It's Gone Too Far

How do you know when your daughter is in trouble? Adolescence is filled with extreme highs and extreme lows, so how do you know when to be concerned about your adolescent daughter?

In general, there are basic warning signs parents can look for to see if their daughter is having difficulties. These warning signs are not evident with every child in every situation but any or all of them should throw up red flags for parents.

If you daughter is very moody at times and "normal" at other times you should be slightly concerned, but more than likely her moodiness is simply the result of being an adolescent. It is important though, to keep a watchful eye and be aware of other signs such as being consistently down, depressed, or upset. This may signal to you that there is something going on that warrants further attention.

Excessive anger toward parents, other family members, and friends is usually covering up a deeper fear or problem.

Withdrawing from parents and friends or outside activities is a big one. This usually is indicative of something deeper going on.

Grades that are slipping can be a sign of being involved in an unhealthy relationship with a boyfriend or girlfriend. Accompanied by withdrawal from friends and family, falling grades is a definite red flag. This could indicate your daughter is falling into a depressed state or is losing site of her future.

Excessive weight loss in a short time can be a red flag. Accompanied by obsession with food or avoidance of food, excessive weight loss may be an indication of a potential eating disorder. Excessive weight gain may be a sign of your daughter being unable to deal with stress in a healthy way. Instead of talking about what is bothering her she may be turning to food to comfort her and avoiding the pain that consumes her.

Promiscuity can be a sign to parents that your daughter is not feeling competent or confident in herself. She is trying to gain acceptance and competence by aligning herself with the negative female role models on television and in movies who seem to get the guy because of their appearance and what they "put out." Seeking out physical intimacy by dressing a certain way or acting a certain way in exchange for feeling loved begins a detrimental cycle. This may be Dad's cue to become reconnected emotionally and physically with his daughter. Refer to chapter 2 and chapter 4 for some tips regarding how dads can positively effect their daughters' lives.

These are just a few warning signs that should alert you to potentially bigger problems. Remember that you have to allow yourself to put aside your own difficult and hectic life to recognize what may be subtle signs. If you do not make an effort to become consciously aware of your daughter's state of mind, you will miss an opportunity to help your daughter through a very difficult time. This process can be time consuming and frustrating at times but it is better to be preventative than have to deal with the full-blown problem later. In some cases, the longer the signs go unnoticed, the deeper your daughter falls into this state of mind or condition, and the harder it is to bring her back to a healthy mindset. The reason is that, at some level, how your daughter is behaving works for her. It may not be healthy and it may actually in some cases be killing her, but on some level it is meeting her needs. The longer this is allowed to go on the more difficult it is to convince your daughter that something else, something more positive, will meet her needs even more.

As you read through the next seven sections you should notice a common thread which links all of these conditions. Low self-esteem and lack of healthy coping mechanisms can lead your daughter down an unhealthy and unhappy path. It is imperative that parents involved in raising children understand the great responsibility that lies before them. Give your daughter a chance by helping her develop her self-esteem. Show her the importance of dealing with problems in a healthy constructive manner.

We are going to discuss in detail some of the problems or conditions your adolescent daughter is dealing with. The following are the most "popular" of the afflictions. And please, if you suspect your daughter is struggling with any of these problems, do not hesitate to contact your pediatrician or a family therapist to help remedy the problem. Whatever you do, do not think these things could not happen to your daughter because they can and they will if your daughter is struggling on the inside and does not know a more healthy way to deal with her pain.

Depression

Mary Pipher, author of *Reviving Ophelia*, describes depression as, "grieving for the lost self." Young girls suffering from depression internalize their struggles with the issues they are facing as adolescents. This results in feelings of worthlessness, inadequacy, and incompetence. Feeling down is a normal occurrence for everyone as long as you can lift yourself back up. Depression becomes lethal when you feel you just cannot or do not know how to get yourself going anymore.

Young girls who are depressed can exhibit anger, lethargy, and apathy toward life. Trying to meet society's expectations, her parents' expectations, and her own expectations can be debilitating for some individuals. It is no wonder kids get depressed these days. We expect our children to meet certain expectations but rarely do parents ever teach their children healthy coping mechanisms when the pressure gets too great. It is important to make sure you are practicing positive coping mechanisms so you can be a good example for your child.

It is paramount to teach our children to understand and recognize their depression. Parents and teachers should stress to children that if they are not feeling valued by others, they must look inside themselves for validation.

Depressed individuals turn to different outlets to gain this sense of competence or to ease their uncontrollable pain. A depressed adolescent may turn to drugs or alcohol to ease her pain. Food can be a panacea for many. Promiscuity can be a result of being depressed and wanting validation from an outside source. Suicide attempts may be an alternative for some adolescents if they feel there is no way out.

Depression is an underlying cause of eating disorders, self-mutilation, drug and alcohol abuse, unhealthy relationships, promiscuity, and suicide. It is essential to find the cause of the depression, which more than likely is low self-esteem, and treat the condition. Then it is imperative to encourage your child to develop healthy coping mechanisms, which they will use well into adulthood. If you feel your daughter is depressed and cannot pull herself out of this darkness, seek out the aid of a trained therapist or counselor to help you understand what you are dealing with at home and how to cope with it.

Eating Disorders

Eating disorders are running rampant in the United States. In the 80s and 90s there has been an explosion of these conditions. It may be in part to the impossible standards we set for ourselves based on the media image of what we "should" look like. Consider this: twenty to twenty-five years ago the average model was 5 feet 6 inches tall and weighed in the 150s. Today, the average model is 5 feet 10 inches tall and weighs 110 to 115 pounds. Realistically only 5 to 10 percent of the population is predisposed to this thinness. But unfortunately, our daughters do not know that fact. And in combination with a mom who is constantly making negative comments about her body, it's no wonder young girls experience so many negative issues with food.

Eating disorders are also a result of the child's desire to have complete control over something in her life when every thing else seems out of whack.

I became extremely concerned about eating disorders when talking to one teen about the topic. She admitted to me that she was anorexic for a short time but was able to pull herself out of it when she felt food was controlling her life. First, I tried to instill in her how proud she should be of herself for getting her control back because many girls aren't able to defeat their condition on their own, and some never win the battle. Then I became curious and asked her why she thought she fell into the food trap in the first place. She responded by telling me that in health class when the topic of eating disorders was discussed, it seemed as though giving up food for awhile was a viable option for losing weight. This young woman felt that eating disorders were almost glorified, and not condemned, in her class. She responded with a typical teenage answer, "Everyone tried it after we studied it in health class. Everyone was either throwing up or starving themselves for weeks." This disturbed me greatly.

Let us explore the eating disorders themselves and discuss how parents and other adults can help young girls from falling victim to these conditions.

Anorexia Nervosa

Anorexia is an eating disorder which consists of starving oneself, in some cases to death. Statistics reveal that 15 to 20 percent of anorexics eventually die from the horrendous toll the profound weight loss had on their bodies.

Anorexia typically begins in early adolescence. Girls begin to be obsessed with food and dieting. They typically hate their bodies and they experience an "extreme self-induced weight loss," says Dr. Julie White, orator of the audiotape, *How to Build Self Esteem in Your Daughter*. According to Dr. White, anorexics feel just right or even fat when they are extremely thin.

There are many speculations about what causes a child to become anorexic. Each individual has her own underlying conscious or subconscious reasons. One theory Dr. White mentions is girls become anorexic because they are ambivalent about growing up and becoming an adult female. By controlling their weight to an extreme, their breasts never fully develop and their bodies remain small, almost as if to say, "I'm not here. I do not exist. I am not important."

Another reason cited in most of the materials I read and listened to is the control issue. An anorexic feels that she does not have any control over her life. Dr. Pipher states, "she is essentially saying (to parents) 'you see, you can't control my every move' and to society, 'I can be thinner than you want me to be. I am in control of what I eat and you can't make me eat more.'"

Who becomes anorexic? Statistics reveal that anorexia is most prevalent in white, bright, high-achieving families. Authors of *Bulimarexia* report that anorexics come from upwardly mobile families where moms are over involved and dads are preoccupied with work out of the home.

Anorexics have low self-esteem and wish to gain approval. And in times of stress, girls with anorexia turn away from food, which is the opposite of bulimics who in times of stress, turn to food for comfort.

Part of the problem is that the early weight loss is often noticed and the anorexic receives compliments from peers and even family members. Boys may begin to notice them and these girls become convinced that thinner has to be better.

Initial signs of anorexia are girls who always say they just ate or ate earlier and aren't hungry. They tend to obsess about exercise, food, and dieting. As the disease progresses physical signs manifest as a distended abdomen and fine lifeless hair. Menstruation ceases. Anorexics become weak and more susceptible to infections.

If you believe your daughter is anorexic do not try to force her to eat. This will make her resist your intervention even more. The best thing to do is to consult you pediatrician and arrange for your daughter to see a counselor and a nutritionist. The hardest part for parents who have a tendency to be controlling is to give up the control and to allow your daughter to make herself better. It is the job of the therapist and the nutritionist to influence your daughter toward realizing that anorexia is not her friend. This horrible disease has made promises to her like being beautiful and feeling wonderful that it has not and cannot fulfill. Your daughter has to turn on the anorexia herself in order to heal the underlying issues, Dr. Pipher states.

Bulimia

Bulimia, unlike anorexia, tends to begin in later adolescence, even college.

Bulimia is characterized by the binge/purge cycle. These young women will stuff themselves with food uncontrollably and later purge, or vomit, use laxatives, or fast to keep from gaining weight or as a mechanism to lose weight. Some resources say that bulimia is the most common eating disorder among young women.

Mary Pipher states, these girls, "have sold their soul for the perfect body." Bulimia, like anorexia, is a result of our society's obsession with thinness. Women are continually striving for the perfect body. At first, controlling the binge/purge cycle can be accomplished, but most bulimics find themselves being unable to control the urge to purge. This activity fills the need for the young girl. The immediate gratification with food to relieve stress, depression, or to escape leads to the purging so the bulimic can feel relaxed and not guilty about the food she ate.

Bulimics have low self-esteem and some essential personal needs are not being met, so they turn to binging and purging for control, acceptance, and achievement. One problem with bulimics is that they are very hard to spot. Most of them are a normal weight. They do not avoid eating. We may even reinforce their problem by complimenting them on a recent weight loss.

Physical signs of bulimia include a loss of enamel on their teeth from the stomach acids that are thrown up. The index finger may have a scar from the mouth acids when she is continually sticking her finger down her throat. Esophageal lesions can occur. Gastrointestinal problems are common. And purging can create deadly chemical imbalances that may lead to a heart attack.

Some groups of females are more at risk than others. Those at greater risk are gymnasts, dancers, actresses, and models. Any competition or occupation that implies that gaining weight will have a detrimental effect on your performance puts a young woman at risk.

If you suspect your daughter is a bulimic, contact your pediatrician and seek out a qualified therapist and nutritionist for your daughter. Their jobs are to help your daughter best this horrible addiction. Make sure you are encouraging validation of oneself instead of looking for validation elsewhere, and take a look at your life and see if you are modeling effective and healthy coping mechanisms. If not, do a little work on yourself and you will help your daughter tremendously. Overeaters Anonymous (OA) is also a good source to contact if your daughter is having trouble controlling her eating. Many people assume OA is only for overweight individuals but instead this organization helps people take control of their eating. Binging in bulimia represents a loss of control. Therefore these individuals may benefit from OA.

Overeating

Overeating is also a very common eating disorder that your daughter can begin in adolescence.

At a time when acceptance from your peers ranks at the top of the list, being overweight can be horribly painful for your daughter. Unfortunately, our society is not very kind to overweight individuals. We tend to judge them as lazy, dumb, and unmotivated individuals. Because of this attitude we have as adults, this cruelty spills over to our children and if they are overweight they feel inadequate. If they are not overweight, kids do not seem to have any problems making fun of overweight individuals right in front of them. As adults, we usually talk about overweight individuals behind their backs which maybe helps us rationalize why we do it. Of course, if they do not hear us make fun of them it cannot hurt them, right? Wrong. Overweight individuals do hear you and it hurts deeply. Children who are overweight are deeply affected as well. Most kids do not have enough life experience to know that those who make fun of others are insecure themselves. Kids do not understand that this is a person's unhealthy coping mechanism, which helps them feel good about themselves at the expense of others. Overweight children internalize the experience, which causes pain and causes them to eat more.

Overeaters tend to have low self-esteem. They turn to food to satisfy their need for love, acceptance, and approval. There could be a control issue with overeaters as well. They may feel that with everything else going crazy in the world, at least they can control what they eat and for a short while this makes them feel good. Their coping mechanism is immediate gratification instead of delayed gratification. These children may or may not need therapeutic intervention. This is up to the parents and the pediatrician. But a trip to a counselor and a nutritionist may help your overweight child.

As a parent with a child who overeats, do not fool yourself and think food is the issue, because it's not. But there are things you can do around your house to eliminate the temptation to overeat. Keep healthy food around the house and get rid of the chips and candy bars. Encourage physical activity by going biking or walking together. Teach your daughter to eat to live, not live to eat.

For all eating disorders, parents first need to address the child's self-esteem issue. Parent should look at themselves first and see what they are possibly not giving to our child. Are you physically or emotionally disconnected? Ask your child. She will tell you what you are doing wrong. Listen past the criticism and try to meet your child's needs. Model appropriate coping mechanisms, stop talking about your weight, teach your children not to judge by looks, and teach your daughter to judge her own body by healthy guidelines.

All of this may take some time and energy but it is worth it. After all, your children are the most precious of all gifts you have ever received.

Unhealthy Relationships

Many resources have been printed in the last five years about the differences between men and women. Most will agree that for women, relationships define their lives. How women are getting along in their relationships has a direct impact on their self-esteem. For men, performance in their career—how good they are at a task—helps shape their self-esteem.

The importance of relationships begins early on in the life of an adolescent girl. Who her friends are, how many friends she has, and whether she is popular or not seem to be of utmost importance to the adolescent girl. One thing that is not so evident and is often overlooked is the importance of the relationship with her family at this time. It certainly does not seem important at the time, but as a young girl reaches adolescence she begins to take her family for granted, especially her parents. She is confident they will always be there so she goes out to develop new relationships with peers, both boys and girls.

This is the time when parents seem to pull away. They are convinced their daughter needs to separate from them in order to be independent so they leave her alone. Or the converse is true, parents are so hurt or frightened by their daughter going off on her own and not needing them anymore that they pull in the reigns too tight and this causes rebellion and resentment.

The point I am trying to make is that you must look at your relationship with your daughter to determine if it is a healthy relationship. If not, you cannot change her. You must change yourself to have any chance to develop a healthy relationship. In chapters 5 and 6 we discussed coping mechanisms and tips on influencing your daughter's behavior by changing what you are doing.

Unhealthy Relationships with Peers

A staggering statistic revealed during an episode of the *Oprah Winfrey Show* states that one in four teenage girls will become a victim of violence from her boyfriend by the time she graduates from high school. This is unbelievable to me. This statistic almost mirrors the finding that one in four adult women will have been assaulted in their lifetime.

What can and should we do about this situation? We should not just zero in on boys here because many times I witness emotional abuse that exists between young girls. Certainly physical abuse is less likely to occur in a girl's relationship with another girl, but verbal and emotional abuse can also be evident.

It is important for us to remember and teach our young girls that just because their actions, whether physical or emotional, do not leave marks we can see, this is still abuse and should not be put up with. As a matter of fact the marks we cannot see, the ones that are inside our heart and soul, are the most difficult to heal. As one psychologist put it, emotional abuse "is a systemic degradation of the soul."

Therefore, any relationship which involves a lack of respect toward your daughter should be of concern to you. And as discussed earlier in this chapter, many times you have no idea what is going on in your daughter's relationships. You may think her boyfriend is the nicest and sweetest thing on this earth because he acts like such a gentleman around you. But maybe to your daughter he is just the opposite. This goes for relationships with your daughter's girlfriends as well. You may never know that your daughter is in an unhealthy relationship if you are not aware of the signs.

The signs of depression, withdrawal, anger, and apathy could be indications of an unhealthy relationship. Pay attention, keep the communication open, and stay connected to your daughter. Then, and only then, will you see the signs if they are there.

Why does your daughter stay in these unhealthy relationships, especially if the relationship involves any kind of abuse? A common theme for all these conditions is low self-esteem. One girl told me, "I didn't think I could do any better." Another, "I didn't think I deserved any better." And yet another, "At least they were giving me some attention and love."

Here are additional signs to teach your daughter to be aware of:

• The person monopolizes your time and attention.
• The person says, "I love you" very early in the relationship.
• You must check in with him frequently.
• He is extremely jealous and possessive.
• He is aggressive in other areas of his life.
• He rough-houses or play wrestles even when you don't want to.
• He blames you for bringing out the worst in him.
• He tries to isolate you from your friends and family.
• He calls you names and embarrasses you in front of others.
• He has an explosive temper or dual personality.
• He uses drugs or alcohol excessively.

In my opinion, every parent should go over this list with his or her daughter early in adolescence. Then you can discuss why these things are unhealthy.

Teenagers often find themselves stuck in these situations because of their low self-esteem, thinking they do not deserve any better and lacking the experience to know better. Because these girls are not experienced with how a healthy relationship should be, especially if their parents have not modeled a healthy relationship, teens often find themselves in this trap with no way out.

Early in the relationship girls may interpret all the attention and jealousy as love. We must teach young girls that jealousy does not equal love. Jealousy equals insecurity. Gavin De Becker, author of *Protecting the Gift*, sums it up by writing, "The fact that a romantic pursuer is relentless doesn't mean you are special. It means that he is troubled."

As the relationship progresses, it is difficult to get out of because these young girls are afraid. In some cases they are afraid of escalating the violence if they leave. In other situations young women may be addicted to this abusive pattern and feel there is nothing out there for them. Whatever the case may be it is important that they have your love and support through the ordeal. This may enable them to have the confidence to move on. Moving on should involve working on themselves. These adolescents should get involved in activities where they feel as though they are accomplishing something. They need to recreate their life which, in most cases, scares the heck of them.

Counseling and your support will help them sort out their strengths and rebuild their life.

If your daughter continues to have problems with the abusive individual either at school or away from school, you have some legal ground to stand on. Contact Break-The-Cycle.org on the internet to find out your legal options for teens. You can also write to:
Dr. Jill Kaplan
30131 Town Center Dr
#280
Laguana Niguel, CA 92677

Gavin de Becker, author of *Protecting the Gift* lists 7 survival signals parents can teach their daughters to help them refrain from getting sucked into an adverse situation which includes unhealthy relationships. These signals are discussed in detail in chapter 8.

SELF-MUTILATION

As I was doing research for this book, I came across this topic and needless to say, it disturbed me. "Self-mutilation can be seen as a concrete interpretation of our culture's injuncture to young women to carve themselves into culturally acceptable pieces," writes Dr. Pipher.

Dr. Pipher states she never saw any clients with this condition until the last five to ten years. Self-mutilation occurs during times of stress when an individual turns on herself with razors, cigarettes to create burns, or knives.

The development of self-mutilation in the 90s may be due to the ever-increasing pressures of girls trying to "carve" themselves into acceptable looking women. It is the extreme of turning on your self and burying your despair inside.

Girls who have no other means of coping with their problems except by turning on themselves is a gruesome thought, but a very real occurrence. And the longer their self-mutilation goes untreated the more difficult it is to treat.

What benefits do these girls get out of hurting themselves? One girl said, "It was the only thing I could do to calm myself down. I guess it relaxes me." After an apparent suicide attempt another girl confided in me, "I really didn't want to die. I just need to get the pain out of me. I wanted to bleed it out." The apparent addiction to physical pain may be due to a release of emotions which they experience from their response to pain. A teen told me, "I kind of feel like I'm floating when it's over. I almost feel numb."

Low self-esteem and a lack of healthy coping mechanisms can lead these girls to harm themselves. But Dr. Mary Pipher has good news. She states, "Most young women respond quickly to guidance about how to stop this behavior and develop more adaptive coping mechanisms." Instead of turning on themselves they learn the benefits of talking about their pain and the stress they are dealing with.

Drug and Alcohol Abuse

Drug and alcohol abuse is relatively common among adolescents. Anytime I have asked a high school-age girl if illegal drugs are apparent at her school, the answer is almost always, yes. According to teens I spoke with, it seems that everyone knows who is dealing, selling, or using drugs.

According to a 1997 study, 82 percent of high school seniors have used alcohol; in comparison, 65 percent have smoked cigarettes; 50 percent have smoked marijuana, and 9 percent have used cocaine.

Use of alcohol and other drugs is associated with the leading causes of death and injury (e.g., motor-vehicle crashes, homicides, and suicides) according to the Centers for Disease Control. Children who use alcohol and other drugs often engage in other risk-taking behavior such as inadequate contraception and physical abuse.

Why are adolescents getting involved in drugs and alcohol at an early age? Unfortunately, there is not only one reason. Depression, low self-esteem, and peer pressure are a few of the reasons I have observed. The attitude that "nothing bad can happen to me" and "everyone is doing it" are common among teens.

Youngsters who are depressed often use alcohol and drugs to medicate themselves. To ease their pain, these youths turn to illegal substances. They lack the appropriate coping mechanisms that would aid them in living a healthy lifestyle.

Interestingly enough, the American Academy of Pediatrics reports that adolescents who are less likely to use alcohol or other drugs are close to their parents emotionally. Other deterrents to alcohol and drug abuse are parents who provide sound, consistent guidance, and siblings who are intolerant of drug use. Adolescents who are expected to comply with clearly understood rules of conduct are also less likely to use drugs or alcohol.

73

Many people with whom I discuss this topic (both adults and teens) insist that experimenting with alcohol is a normal occurrence. It is beyond the scope of this book to agree or disagree with whether experimentation should be tolerated. In my opinion, these statistics speak for themselves. Among teenagers who binge drink, 39 percent say they drink alone; 58 percent drink when they are upset; 30 percent drink when they are bored; and 37 percent drink to feel high according to the Health and Human Services.

It is imperative to supply your children with the tools to resist abusing these substances. As discussed, high self-esteem, clear boundaries, modeling appropriate behaviors, modeling appropriate consumption of alcohol, and teaching your children healthy alternatives to coping with their problems are all key factors in keeping your child from abusing these illegal substances.

If parents still think it is not that important to talk about drug and alcohol abuse consider this: a survey by the Health and Human Services Division revealed that 18 percent of female teens and 39 percent of male teens say it is acceptable for a boy to force sex if the girl is stoned or drunk. Hopefully, your daughter won't be experimenting around these kids.

Suicide

According to the Yellow Ribbon Suicide Prevention web site, suicides among young people nationwide have increased dramatically in recent years. Suicide among 15 to 19 year olds is the second leading cause of death. And even more alarming is that suicide is the sixth leading cause of death for 5 to 14 year olds. Suicide is the fastest growing killer of youth in America.

Girls are four times more likely to attempt suicide, but boys are more apt to succeed. This may be due to the methods more commonly used by each sex. Females tend to take pills whereas boys use more violent methods, such as guns.

Clusters of suicides are becoming more common in adolescents. Clusters are suicides attempted secondary to a suicide in the family or community. Statistics reveal that from twenty to fifty cluster suicide attempts are common after a suicide attempt by a teenager.

Authors Tonia K. Shamoo and Philip Patros state that the following are warning signs that your child may be troubled by suicidal thoughts.

• Change in eating and sleeping habits
• Withdrawal from friends and family and regular activities
• Violent actions, rebellious behavior, or running away
• Drug and alcohol use

- Abrupt, prolonged changes in behavior
- Persistent boredom, difficulty concentrating, or a decline in the quality of schoolwork
- Frequent complaints about physical symptoms, often related to emotions, such as stomachaches, headaches, fatigue, etc.
- Statements such as "I want to kill myself," "I won't be a problem for you much longer," "Nothing matters," or "No one would care if I wasn't here anyway"
- Giving away valued possessions
- Suddenly cheerful after a period of depression

One or more of these signs should not be ignored.

Anytime an adolescent says, "I want to kill myself" ALWAYS take the statement seriously. Intervention by a psychiatrist or other physician is important. Talk to your pediatrician for referrals.

Don't be afraid to talk to your daughter about suicide or depression. Ignoring it will not make it go away and talking about it will NOT put ideas in her head. Your daughter may feel that no one cares or no one understands. By expressing your concern, she may realize that someone really does care. Be observant of any signs listed above as well as any signs related to depression.

When approaching your daughter about suicide you must LISTEN to what she has to say. Encourage her to share her feelings. Refrain from telling her all the reasons she should not commit suicide, and by all means do not tell her that her feelings are foolish or she is being silly. Reassure her that she can be helped and she will have your support at all times.

Follow through by finding help for your daughter. If your pediatrician does not have any referrals, call a suicide hotline in your area for advice. Yellow Ribbon's web site is http://www.yellowribbon.org.

Teen Pregnancy

Are you concerned about your daughter becoming sexually active at a young age? Well, you should be. According to the National Campaign to Prevent Teen Pregnancy, more than four out of ten young women become pregnant at least once before they reached the age of 20. That is nearly 1,000,000 per year or almost 3,000 per day. Eight in ten of these pregnancies are unintended and 80 percent are to unmarried teens. Four in ten girls who first had intercourse at 13 or 14 years old report it was either non-voluntary or unwanted.

Only one third of teen mothers are likely to receive their high school diploma. Eighty percent of unwed teen moms end up on welfare.

What can you do to prevent teenage pregnancy? Statistics show a teen who has a strong emotional attachment to her parents are much less likely to become sexually active at an early age. In other words, be there for your daughter. A dad has a huge impact on his daughter's outlook on sex and sexuality. Dads, don't disappear from your daughter's life, emotionally or physically, because you are uncomfortable with how she is changing. For tips on how dads can positively influence their daughter's lives refer to chapter 3 and chapter 6.

Single moms face a realistic challenge when there is no male role model in their daughter's life. If possible, enlist the help of a grandfather, uncle, or an older brother to provide your daughter with a healthy male role model.

Keeping your daughter involved in extracurricular activities after school can lower her chances of becoming pregnant as a teen. It is well documented that girls involved in athletics are less likely to practice unhealthy risk taking behaviors. Help your daughter find activities where she can gain a sense of accomplishment and begin to value herself.

And finally, do not be afraid to talk to your daughter about sex. Seven out of ten teens reported that they were ready to listen to things their parents thought they were not ready to hear.

NOTE: It is important to encourage your daughter to attend counseling if necessary. There is nothing to be ashamed of as a parent or child. There is no manual on parenting that answers all the questions. Sorting out your thoughts with a therapist can be very beneficial.

It is important to also be realistic. If you or your daughter seek counseling and find the person you are seeing is not right for you, then try someone else. It is important that the person attending counseling sessions be comfortable with their therapist. If you feel uncomfortable, you will be less apt to open up and share your deepest feelings. So do not be discouraged or feel you have to stay with the first person you encounter. Finding the right professional, someone who you or your daughter can relate to, will make all the difference in the world. Remember you cannot expect the counselor to solve your problems for you, but hopefully they will guide you in your struggle to come up with the answers.

Chapter Eight

KEEPING YOUR DAUGHTER SAFE

The following chapter was a late addition. I would be doing a disservice to anyone who read this book had I not included this information. The fact is, teenage girls are the "most victimized segment of the population and the least likely to report a crime," according to Gavin De Becker, author of *Protecting the Gift*. A survey of inmates who have committed violence against young people reported that 75 percent of the victims were girls. Why? Girls offer less resistance and pose less risk than adult females.

When you think about it, this statement makes sense. Even in our "modern" society where women are supposedly treated better than ever before, teenage girls are looked upon as sex objects. I would bet that in the majority of the ten-thousand plus "gentlemen" clubs around the country there is the typical skit of the teenage girl in a school uniform—plaid skirt, saddle shoes, and white shirt licking a lollipop. She obviously is an exotic dancer who strips down to next to nothing and while doing so, feeds the fantasy of every male in attendance that a teenage girl, though innocent, is nothing but a sex object. Prohibited maybe, but still an object of sexual pursuit.

I am not saying that strip clubs are the reason men rape or sexually assault teenage girls. There are obviously plenty of men who attend these establishments and never hurt a female. But men don't need any help in the department of abusing young women. Rape and other sexual crimes are almost always committed by men. Most of these deviant crimes happen to girls under eighteen. Many of these crimes are committed by someone familiar to the girl.

Parents should be cautious about who they allow in their young adolescent daughter's lives. Many times these crimes are committed by a neighbor or friend. These people work their way into your home and life and gain your trust. They are very persuasive. In addition, these people do not resemble scary monsters like children imagine in their minds. Usually these criminals look like everyday people. Their persuasive nature and ability to blend in make them an unlikely threat to your daughter. Don't be fooled. The remainder of this chapter may aid you in picking these people out before they get too close.

How Do You Keep Your Daughter from Becoming a Victim?

This is probably the most important question parents can ask themselves. Can you keep your daughter safe? The truth is parents cannot always keep their daughters safe. This fact leads to many sleepless nights for parents.

What can a parent do? The best way to help keep your daughter safe from sexual predators is to teach her three very important lessons. First, encourage your daughter from a young age to listen to her intuitive self. Second, teach her how to say "No." And third, make her aware of the survival signals and the meaning of privacy and control.

Intuition

Teaching your daughter to listen to her intuitive self means encouraging her to listen to the feeling she gets when she knows something isn't right or when it is right. Help her to understand an uneasy feeling in certain situations is her first line of defense and she should not brush it aside. Your daughter should heed that internal warning and quickly determine if the situation she is about to encounter is safe. Some of the women and girls that I have spoken to who have been raped or sexually assaulted have told me they had an uneasy feeling about where they were or about the person that ended up hurting them. These women ignored their own warnings by rationalizing and in the end they became the victim.

I am not in any way blaming these women for what happened to them. They were victims of a very serious crime. But from every bad situation lessons can be learned. The lesson is, teach your daughter to listen to her intuitive self to avoid situations that may be harmful to her. In addition your daughter should listen to her intuition to determine if a situation is safe and right for her.

One way in which you can encourage her to become conscious of these internal warning signals in simply by asking her how she feels in different situations. For example, when meeting someone new, what was her first impression or feeling about that person? Did she feel comfortable around them or not?

Another example of teaching your daughter to become conscious of her internal warning signals is by asking her in specific circumstances what her initial feelings were. More specifically, if she is going to a party where you are concerned there will be alcohol served, ask her to be conscious of her feelings. If she is offered alcohol and is apprehensive, tell her that the apprehensive feeling is her intuition sending her a signal. Most girls rationalize by saying, "Everyone is doing it. It's no big deal." Or they cave in to peer pressure. Peers may say, "Don't be a wimp," or "Come on, no one will find out." This example applies not only to alcohol, but also drugs, sex, and any other adverse situation a young girl may encounter.

Listening to your intuition is an essential tool when it comes to making the right decision in adverse situations. Many adults have not yet mastered this ability. This ability is inbred in all of us. We simply have to become conscious of this ability in order to use it.

Saying "No"

This sounds so silly. Of course a young girl knows how to say no. She may know how to say no, but guaranteed, an adolescent girl is apprehensive to use this word in appropriate situations. Women in general have a difficult time saying no. It is engrained in us from early on that we should try to please others. We tend to be less likely to ruffle any feathers or make waves for fear of hurting someone else. Women model this to their daughters. Girls subconsciously pick this up at a very young age. This can hurt us in the short run and the long run.

Girls should be able to assert themselves. Sexual predators will often seek out the passive, nonassertive individual as their next victim. They look for someone they know they can control and will be the least resistive to their demands. These disturbed individuals will be more likely to avoid the young girl who asserts herself. Being assertive is a signal to them that this young girl will tell and lead to their demise. As a matter of fact, a powerful sentence to teach your daughter contains only two words, "I'll tell."

Saying no to young suitors is a difficult task as well. Girls and women have a tendency to make up excuses as an attempt to keep from hurting their pursuers feelings. It can be very difficult to say, "No, I do not want to go out with you." Women in real life, and women portrayed in the media teach young women to make up excuses such as, "I'm just not interested in a relationship now." This only encourages the young man because he only hears "now" and believes that there maybe a chance in the future. It is seen time after time in the movies and on television that if a girl says no, she really doesn't mean no. If you try hard enough she will finally give in. Society and the media have taught us that when a man says no, it is final. When a woman says no, it is the beginning of a negotiation.

It is important to teach your daughter to assert herself and be honest. If she eventually gives in, the cycle continues and the other person will not take her seriously. (Sounds like a good parenting tip too!) It is equally as important to explain to your daughter that being assertive may label her as being a bitch, a wimp, or even conceited. However, the alternative is having a daughter who puts herself into very precarious situations with longstanding negative consequences. A parent must explain to their daughter that anyone who calls her these names is insecure. They are either trying to gain control of her, or make her one of them so they can feel better about themselves.

A parent must remember that teaching their daughter to be assertive will undoubtedly result in some heated discussions at home. This is unavoidable but the alternative—

your daughter being passive and therefore, becoming a target—is unacceptable. The key here is to stress that being disrespectful will not be tolerated. When your daughter disagrees with you, you must tell her that you respect her opinion but your opinion differs from hers and this is the way it is going to be. It is important to continue the parent role and not revert to trying to be her friend and spare her feelings. Also, if a parent expects to be treated with respect, the parent must treat the daughter with respect. If a parent yells, screams, or uses obscenities, that parent should not be surprised to hear the same coming from the daughter.

> The following material may give parents the impression that they must teach their daughters to be paranoid of any and every man they ever talk to. The point here and in the following material is that the reality is, girls are at risk of being abused, attacked, molested, raped, and exploited. With this being the case, a consistent reminder to girls to be aware of how they feel about certain situations and people will only help them become more conscious in other areas of their life and spare them the emotional pain associated with these situations. When done consistently and appropriately, teaching your daughter to trust her intuitive self, encouraging her to say no when necessary, and learning these survival signals will be an opportunity to stay connected with your daughter and help in her development as a confident young woman.

The Survival Signals

In the book *Protecting the Gift*, author Gavin de Becker lists seven "Survival Signals." These signals will aid your daughter in recognizing when someone is trying to gain control of her and possibly lead her to a harmful situation. It is imperative to teach your daughter these signals over time. A parent should become aware of the signals to keep their child safe when they are too young to defend themselves. The seven signals are:

- Forced Teaming
- Charm and Niceness
- Too Many Details
- Typecasting
- Loan-sharking
- The Unsolicited Promise
- Discounting the Word No

These signals are what predators use to gain control of the situation. They accomplish this through persuasion. First the individual must persuade the young girl to come with him. The violent crime occurs once he has gained control and gets her to a place where he has accomplished privacy. First, then, it is important for a girl to not relinquish her control.

Forced Teaming

Forced teaming is a way to persuade the potential victim to relate to the possible assailant. Using phrases which imply "We've got something in common," is a way to convince the girl that he is on her side. You may notice forced teaming when the assailant says "now we've done it," "both of *us*," or "how are *we* going to handle this?" He creates a relationship where none really exists.

Good responses to forced teaming would be, "WE are not going to handle this. I am." "Both of us are not involved in this so please leave me alone." "Excuse me sir, there is no 'we' involved here, so please stop bothering me." Granted, these responses may seem rude, but they can stop an assailant in his tracks. Wouldn't a parent rather her daughter seemed rude than taken advantage of by criminal?

Many different kinds of people may perform forced teaming for no deviant reason. They may be trying to establish rapport. But as Mr. De Becker states, "when applied by a stranger, forced teaming is always inappropriate."

Charm and Niceness

People seeking control are always nice and charming, at first. Control is their motive. Parents must teach their daughters that charm is not necessarily a good thing. It is essential to recognize when being charming is out of place or inappropriate. Many times the internal signals which we have discussed before will help a girl determine the intent of the "nice, charming" person. It is not unusual for parents to think that a daughter's boyfriend or girlfriend is "so nice" and wonderful. This can cloud the parent's judgement and they can miss important signals if there is in fact an unhealthy relationship between the two.

Too Many Details

This technique helps the assailant distract the individual he is trying to control. He may use too many details to make the young girl more comfortable with him. In essence he is trying to get her to lose sight of the fact that he is a total stranger and should be analyzed cautiously.

Often this technique is used by the assailant because he is making sure that he does not seem to be a threat. What he is saying may sound normal to you, but to him it doesn't sound so credible and that is why he keeps talking. A young girl must remember, this is a complete stranger and if he is trying to hard, then something is up.

Typecasting

Typecasting involves slightly insulting an individual to get them to prove him wrong. An example of this is "You would never do something so crazy, would you?" Another could be, "You are probably pretty straight laced, aren't you?"

The assailant is attempting to get the teenager to say, "Oh yes I would," or "No, I'm not so straight-laced." This would allow him to convince her to take the next step which may involve leaving with him or allowing him to do something she that would normally make her uncomfortable. An adolescent may not want to seem "out of it" or a "goody-two-shoes." Therefore, it is imperative for her to recognize this tactic and use her best line of defense, silence. She should just ignore the question or comment as though it hasn't been said. Another way to handle it would be to say, "I am not going to answer that question because it was so inappropriate," if silence is not an option. Don't forget, the typecaster doesn't actually believe what he is saying. He simply thinks it will work.

Loan-sharking

Unfortunately, in today's society we have to be conscious of what anyone's motive may be. Loan-sharking can be described as doing something for someone in order for them to feel like they owe you.

Most often people who offer to help you when you have not solicited their help are just being kind. But it is important to teach a girl to be cautious (not paranoid) of someone who offers them help for no reason. If the situation appears safe and appropriate and the person doesn't exhibit any additional signs we are discussing, then most likely they are just being kind. But loan-sharking lumped together with other signals spells trouble.

The Unsolicited Promise

A promise is no guarantee. It reveals intent, but is not reliable. Promising something to an adolescent is often times misconstrued by the adolescent as the undeniable truth. A parent must explain to their daughter that a promise from a stranger should always be approached with caution. The stranger is trying to convince you of something with no intention of keeping their promise. He is only trying to convince her of something. They are inessence saying, "Okay, I know you don't trust me so I am going to promise you something so you will trust me."

Gavin de Becker's advice is when someone promises you something you should say in your head or out loud, "You're right, I am hesitant to trust you. Thank you for pointing it out."

Discounting the Word "No"

As discussed earlier in this chapter, "no" can be a very powerful word. But what happens when a person continues to pursue the situation even after your refusal? This is a classic example of wanting to control someone.

Discounting the word no by a stranger or someone you know is a huge red flag. It is evident that this person doesn't respect your wishes. A young girl must learn the importance of sticking to her guns when she says no. If she backs down she relinquishes control to the other person and that person is empowered.

Teach your daughter to recognize that when someone ignores "no" they are trying to gain control over her. Encourage her to ask herself, "Why is this person trying to control me?" The best choice would be to get away from this person, but if that is not possible, a very loud and direct, "I said no!" may be necessary.

If a girl finds herself in a situation with a boyfriend or man where they are alone and he makes advances that she is uncomfortable with, it is important for her to feel comfortable saying no. If the person persists by utilizing some of the other techniques we have discussed it is important to reiterate "no" is still the answer. If the person attempts physical violence it is important to attempt to get away any way she can. Yelling, kicking, screaming, whatever it takes.

As an aside, I believe that every female should learn some form of self-defense. In a world where one out of four women will be assaulted to some degree in their lifetime, self defense classes should be a requirement for girls. To find a self-defense program in your area some good places to start would be Kidpower 1-800-467-6997, IMPACT for kids 1-800-345-5425, or a local self defense studio.

Privacy and Control

We have already established that one criteria necessary for an individual to cause harm to someone is gaining control. The second criteria for the assailant to carry out the crime is he must gain privacy.

Privacy can be a field far away from anyone, a person's home with no one home, or a room in a house sometimes even when people are home. The level of privacy needed really depends on how easily controlled the victim is. Adolescent and teenage girls without proper preparation can be controlled more easily than adult females. This was the case when I was a young girl. I was molested by a neighbor down the street. All he needed was a dark room to accomplish what he set out to do. Although I was quite young and am not sure of all the details, there could have been others in the house

83

when he molested me because I did not utter a sound. I was too afraid to say a word at the time or after the incident. The incident occurred when I was seven and I never revealed my secret to anyone until I was nineteen.

The key here is to educate young girls to try to prevent them from getting into a situation they cannot get out of. Younger adolescents probably will not understand many of the survival signals with exception of the unsolicited promise, and discounting the word "no". They should be made aware of the fact that if anyone tries to get them to do something and tells them they can't tell their parents or anyone else that they are up to something inappropriate. A parent must encourage a daughter to talk to them about anyone who makes her feel uneasy or tells her to keep a secret. If the perpetrator tries to convince the young girl not to tell by saying he will hurt the parents or the parents will be disappointed or mad at her the girl must feel comfortable coming to tell the parent what the perpetrator said. The only way this is accomplished is by telling the child over and over that they can come talk to you about anything that anyone says. It is important to make her aware that if someone says they will hurt their parents if she doesn't do what he says, this person is lying and you should be told about it. Reiterate to the young girl that the person will not be able to hurt you.

It is essential to avoid discounting the young girl if she does come to you about anything that has made her feel uncomfortable. This is true even if you don't think it is very important, such as tattling on someone. Instead of saying you shouldn't tattle on someone and reprimanding her, a better response would be, "Thank you for letting me know. I will keep an eye on him/her."

The reason you should not discipline, or should really downplay, tattling is because you are sending a message to this little girl not to tell on someone if they are doing something they perceive as bad. It also will conflict with the you-can-tell-me-anything message. If the tattling persists and it really isn't information that the girl needs to report, you can explain the reason why it is okay for the other child to do what they are doing. And encourage the young girl to play somewhere else if it this action disturbs her.

Another safety tip for school aged children would be to have a certain word or phrase that you would give to a person to say to the child if there is an emergency and the parent cannot pick them up from school or daycare. This may keep any unwanted adult from trying to remove your child from a playground or picking the child up while walking home from school. Most daycare centers and schools require parents to call or contact the teacher if someone else is picking up their child.

Additional information that a parent should teach their child is what is inappropriate touching. A parent should explain that it is inappropriate for someone else to touch the child as well as someone else encouraging the child to touch them in areas covered by a bathing suit. For more information on exactly how to explain this to your child, I would recommend reading *Protecting the Gift* by Gavin de Becker.

Older adolescents (twelve- to fifteen-year-olds) can be introduced to the rest of the survival signals. They will not fully comprehend them so it is important to review the signals frequently. For example, after meeting a stranger and talking to them ask them to try to identify if the stranger was using any of the techniques we have discussed. Make it some sort of game between the two of you so the girl would be more apt to participate. This will also make the parent conscious of recognizing the techniques. This, coupled with teaching them to listen to their body's internal signals will enable the teenager to become more in tune with herself and the people around her.

Fifteen-to eighteen-year-olds may have an easier time recognizing the survival signals. They will need practice also, so a parent should sparingly ask if they have encountered any of the signals throughout the day at school amongst their friends and teachers. Again, attempt to make it a fun activity.

Role Playing

Role playing is discussed in a previous chapter, but I feel it is important to discuss it in this chapter as well. It would be a good idea to role play with your children certain situations that they may encounter at different times in their lives. For example, you are going to the mall during the Christmas rush with your eight-year-old daughter. It is a good idea sometime before you leave or even on the way in the car, to role play a situation she may encounter if the two of you would get separated. A parent could make a game out of this so you are not scaring the child but instead, preparing the child for an adverse situation.

Younger teens are constantly bombarded with new decisions about taking drugs, drinking alcohol, and having sexual relationships. Many have never encountered these situations before, so role playing BEFORE they encounter the situation would give them an edge. They may feel more confident making the more responsible decision if they have gone over it with their parent before. Parents should not be naive. Every child will encounter some type of peer pressure to participate in the situations listed.

Older teens should be reminded of the survival signals and if, they are familiar with role playing with a parent, they will be apt to approach you or their friends about helping them work a situation out ahead of time.

A key element that should not be missed here is even though parents will be met with some opposition as a daughter gets older, that doesn't mean they should retreat and exit from their daughter's life for awhile. Instead, the parent should be available to their daughter on her terms as she stumbles through adolescence. An adolescent may be resistive to role playing or understanding the survival signals at first, but in the long run they will be much more aware of their own feelings and the actions of people around them. So parents, don't give up. Stay connected to your daughters. This way you have done all you can to keep your daughter safe.

Chapter Nine

LETTERS TO PARENTS FROM THEIR DAUGHTERS

Dear Mom,

Although my time is often strictly confined to the constraints of sports, homework, meetings, work, and school, I do think about you...more often than you think. It is not often that I get the opportunity to reflect upon our relationship, but that does not mean that it is not always affecting me.

Mom, you are the strongest, bravest, most determined woman that I know. I am proud to have been raised by you. Your childhood proved to be one of your greatest challenges in life, but I believe that it has only made you stronger.

Through your experiences, I was able to understand and appreciate so much more in life than many of those around me. You are an inspiration to me and to all people because you represent a caring, loving, devoted mother who has sacrificed so much for the mere happiness of your children.

Your faith in me when I made wrong choices, your determination to see that we never need for anything, and your unconditional love are what make you my mom. I can only hope that my own children will someday appreciate me as much as I appreciate you.

All I can say Mom is, thank you. Thank you for caring, for giving me space, for comforting me, for believing in me, and most of all, for giving me the opportunity to know and love one of the most beautiful people I've ever know.

I love you and I am grateful every day for you.

Dear Mom,

You have raised me to be a strong, intelligent, young woman. You've taught me everything from cooking and cleaning to loving and believing.

If I had to change one thing about you it would be for you to express your own opinion. Sometimes I feel I cannot ask you a question or for advice and get your honest opinion. I think Dad vastly influences your opinion. It is not so much that he forces you to think a certain way, but it is more an issue of self-esteem.

Feel good about yourself and your opinion. Stand up for what you believe in. No one will look down upon you.

What I mean is, if Dad likes a certain type of music you would too. Even with politics, if Dad were a Democrat, you would be one, too. I think this characteristic is the main reason for many of our fights. If you try to work on your "flaws" I promise I'll try to work on mine. Hopefully, if we both work on it, our relationship will change for the better.

Dear Mom and Dad,

This letter is kind of hard to write. I was interviewed for this book and then asked to write a letter about listening. Honestly, I really don't think you ever listen to me. Whenever I come to you with a problem, you usually cut me off and tell me your opinion before I get through telling you my whole problem. It seems like you don't care what I have to say. Most of our talks end up in fights. I know you think I am disrespectful or spoiled because I heard you guys say that behind my back.

I just want you to hear my side of things and then maybe you will understand me a little better. I just want you to think that I am important and maybe I have something to say that would surprise you. Maybe you might think I'm smart or something.

When you don't listen it makes me want to do things that will make you mad. I don't know why cuz I will just get in trouble. When you don't listen to me it makes me think you don't love me.

So please, just once, listen to what I have to say.

Thanks.

(This letter was from an adolescent girl who felt she was not heard. Her situation at home was very tense. She felt her parents were really getting on her nerves. She also realized that she was probably getting on her parents nerves as well.)

Dad,

I was asked to write this letter because I have noticed that you are not around as much as you used to be. You and I used to laugh a lot. You would totally crack me up.

Lately, it's like you don't want to be around me anymore. If I did something to make you mad, I'm sorry.

I miss your hugs. I miss just going for an ice cream for no reason. I miss talking to you about anything.

I hope I didn't do anything to make you mad. I know I do a lot of stuff with my friends. I hope that doesn't make you mad.

Can we be friends again Dad?

(This letter is the result of an interview with one teen that felt she was losing her father. She didn't know why, but as she put it, "all of a sudden he wasn't there anymore. I really felt alone.")

ARE YOU MY MOTHER?

Many people look at their mothers and find beauty and a role model for when they mature. Mothers are supposed to be caring and loving, and give a daughter hope when they feel empty inside. But what happens when the mother you need for protection and kindness seems miles away? Where does a daughter go to have questions answered, hugs received, kind words spoken, and love given?

My mother was not there for me in my young adulthood. My childhood is a faint dream of harsh realities. The lessons I learned were from people that I made a mistake loving. I wanted love from anywhere because I didn't find it in my mother's arms. The people who taught me about so-called love and respect are the ones that hurt me the most. I yearned for love from anywhere and the next thing I knew I was being used in all ways possible. I found myself in a relationship based on sex and lies. I forgave so easily because losing another person would hurt too much. I was cheated on, verbally abused, and sent on an emotional whirlwind.

My mother lingers in the back of my mind and the hope that someday I could love her always pulls at my soul. I try to think of the future and wonder if she will be a part of it.

I wish that we had a relationship that was open and full of love. I want all those terrible things in the past to go away, but they won't. I want to know why she wanted to hurt me so bad, and why she didn't see the pain I felt.

(This is an excerpt from a teenager's reflection who feels she traveled down the wrong path because of her relationship with her parents. Most of her anger is directed toward her mother.)

I am kinda scared. Ever since my parents split up I feel angry inside. I know they told me once that it wasn't my fault, but sometimes I still believe that it was. Sometimes I think it was my dad's fault. Some days I think it's my mom's fault. I guess I'm pretty confused.

My parents don't talk about it much so I don't either. When I'm with Dad I know he tries hard to be fun and pretend he knows what I'm going through. When I'm with Mom sometimes the stupidest things make me mad at her. And then I get into trouble for being a brat.

My feelings inside are all messed up. I just want to talk about it, but I'm afraid. Sometimes they ask me if I'm okay and I say yes because I don't want them to worry about me. I know they are very busy. Inside I want to say that it hurts, but sometimes I don't know what "it" is.

A lot of friends at school have parents that are divorced. They seem okay with it. What is wrong with me? I wish we could all be together again, but I guess it wasn't so good before they broke up. But at least we would be together and then maybe I wouldn't feel so messed up.

(This letter was written by a young adolescent coping with a recent divorce.)

Dad,

From little girl on, you have always been my biggest supporter. It's hard for me to imagine where I would be today had I not received your guidance and support. Through the highs and lows, you were always there at my side. As I look back on some of the more difficult years of my life (undoubtedly my teenage years), I realize how instrumental you were in keeping the peace between Mom and me. I could never thank you enough Dad, for all those times you were there to advise me on how to handle yet another confrontation with Mom, or to enlighten me in my ignorance about what I had done to make her mad and how I could best get myself out of the jam.

At times you truly were my salvation, and for this I am eternally grateful. Just like when I was a young child, I still look up into your eyes and see a gentle caring man who is compassionate, understanding, and full of love. I see a man who has taught me some of the greatest of life's lessons and who for these reasons I hold in the highest esteem. I'm proud to say I'm truly my daddy's girl. I love you with all my heart.

A letter to my parents:

Mom and Dad, I am sure I was a handful when I went through my adolescent years. I know that I was much more of a challenge at times than either of my brothers.

As I look back on it now, I am so sorry about the way I treated you Mom. You gave and gave. And I was more focused on my friends than I was on your feelings. I do remember feeling guilty for things that I had said. But I never seemed to have the words to express my feelings.

Now I have the words, and I want to say that I am sorry for any unnecessary pain I may have caused. I can look back and analyze why I acted the way I did, but the most important thing to me now is that you both know how much I appreciate all the sacrifices you made for us.

You taught me about unconditional love, respect, and boundaries. You taught me to aim high and go after my dreams. You both are great role models. I believe I have the best of both of you in me.

Thank you for all that you have given me. Without your support and encouragement in my life I know I would have never thought I could write this book or achieved the goals I have so far in my life. I am hopeful that parents will read this and realize there is hope for a happy and healthy relationship with their daughter because they are an essential part of their daughter's life.

I apologize for any pain I may have caused. But thank you again for loving me anyway.

Sincerely,
Your daughter,
Stacey

BIBLIOGRAPHY

American Association of University Women. Shortchanging Girls, Shortchanging America. Washington D.C. 1991. **Permission granted from AAUW to reprint statistics relating to their 1991 research study.

Baile, Susan, PhD. *"Building Self Esteem in Your Child"* (Audio tape). Boulder, CO: CareerTrack, 1992.

Begel, Dave. *Bringing Up Emily*. Chicago, Il.: Turnbull & Willoughby, 1986.

Boskind-White, Marlene, PhD. and William C. White Jr., PhD. *Bulimarexia*. New York: W.W. Norton and Co., 1991.

Centers for Disease Control, "Alcohol and Other Drug Use Among High School Students-United States, 1990," *Morbidity and Mortality Weekly Report*, Nov. 1991.

Covey, Stephen. *Seven Habits of Highly Effective Families*. New York: Golden Books, 1997.

Covey, Stephen. *Seven Habits of Highly Effective People*. New York: Simon & Schuster, 1989.

DeBecker, Gavin. *Protecting the Gift*. New York: The Dial Press., 1999.

Debold, Elizabeth, Marie Wilson, and Idelisse Malave. *Mother Daughter Revolution*. New York: Addison-Wesley Publishing Co., 1993.

Friday, Nancy. *My Mother My Self*. New York: Delta Trade Paperbacks, 1997.

Gray, John, PhD. *Men Are From Mars, Women Are From Venus*. New York: Harper Collins, 1992.

Lerner, Harriet, PhD. *The Mother Dance*. New York: Harper Collins, 1998.

Lidz, Theodore. *The Person: His Development Throughout the Life Cycle*. New York: Basic Books, 1968.

McGraw, Phil, PhD. *Life Strategies*. New York: Hyperion Books, 1999.

National Campaign to Prevent Teen Pregnancy 1997. "Whatever Happened to Childhood? The Problem of Teen Pregnancy in the United States." Washington D.C.

OIG, Health and Human Services, "Drinking Habits, etc."

OIG, Heath and Human Services, "Dangerous and Deadly Consequences."

95

Orenstein, Peggy. *School Girls*. New York: Doubleday, 1994.

Phillips, Deborah. *How To Give Your Child a Great Self-Image*. New York: Random House, 1989.

Shamoo, Tonia K., and Philip Patros. *I Want to Kill Myself*. Massachusetts, 1990.

White, Julie, PhD. *Building Self-Esteem in Your Daughter*. (Audio tape). Boulder, CO: CareerTrack, 1995.

Wright, H. Norman. *Always Daddy's Girl*. Ventura, CA: Regal Books, 1989.